Endorsements

Marv Newell blends a solid Biblical study with his mission experience into a popular resource on the Great Commission. You can hear the teacher in Marv, urging us to clarify, go deeper and stretch our thinking. So be careful! These truths are too important to ignore or merely read for head knowledge. We must apply them and act...NOW!

Greg Parsons
General Director, U.S. Center for World Mission

No matter how often you have studied the Great Commission-or how well you feel you understand it - Marv Newell's illuminating book will open your eyes to new insights. Marv combines careful study of the text with practical reflections on pressing missiological issues. Blending his experiences as missions teacher, field missionary and missions association director, Marv brings valuable multiple perspectives to his examination of the text. Whether you are a seasoned missionary or are first exploring the implications of Christ's commission, you will benefit from *Commissioned*.

Dr. Steve Strauss
Professor of Missions, Dallas Theological Seminary

This careful study of the comprehensive teaching of the five "commission" passages recorded in sacred Scripture is excellent. The cumulative impact of the five occasions (not synoptic, but separate and sequential) when Christ mandates us to reach the nations is powerful. *Commissioned* is a great book for classroom study and personal motivation, written by a person who has lived what it teaches.

Dr. George Murray
Chancellor, Columbia International University, SC

Marv has done a great service in providing a timely message to the church at a time when she has blurred her focus and perspective. Instead of being preoccupied with what appear to be more important issues but which are in fact lesser ones—global warming, AIDS, poor children, affordable housing, and short-term projects, Marv reminds us that Jesus left His followers just a few things to focus on—our final assignment. As others have said, Jesus' last command should be our first priority. Shouldn't we set our agenda after His? Marv's book helps us see what Jesus said was most important and how we can wrestle with Great Commission issues in our 21st-century context. I highly recommend this book and urge it to be shared widely.

Dr. Monroe "Monnie" Brewer
President, National Association of Mission Pastors (NAMP)

As a missionary and the son of missionaries, I always assumed I understood the Great Commission. Marv Newell's *Commissioned: What Jesus Wants You to Know as You Go* awakened me with a jolt to how much I've missed! It's as if I've taken an old piece of furniture to the appraiser and discovered that it's worth millions. Newell's scholarly and compelling elucidation of Christ's "marching orders" to the church brings the big picture, and my role in it, back into crystal clear focus. Don't let the 'Great Commission' be your great 'blind spot' any longer. Read this great book!

Steve Richardson
President, Pioneers-USA

As cultural trends and forces attempt to shift the mission of the Church today Marv Newell fires a flare of theology into the air. Biblically-centered, convicting and inspiring, *Commissioned* illumines the path for all to see the primacy of the evangelistic mandate in God's plan. Few books deliver such clarity, balance and practical guidance for those engaged in the Lord's work.

Dr. Dan Wicher
President, CAM International

Marv has provided the Church with a fresh, biblically-grounded, and missiologically-guided book to assist us in understanding the essential elements of the Great Commission. He exegetes and synthesizes the biblical texts with the mind of a theologian and the heart of a missionary. I highly recommend

Commissioned to anyone wanting an excellent understanding of how Jesus' first century words apply to the 21st century world. Get this book; read it; and apply it!

Dr. J. D. Payne
Director of the Church Planting Center
Southern Baptist Theological Seminary, Louisville, KY

In these days when there is so much debate and confusion about what it means to be missional and to be on mission, Marv Newell's *Commissioned* is a clarion call for the disciples of Jesus to return to the simplicity of the parting instructions given to us by our Lord and Savior.

Dr. Timothy R. Sisk
Chair & Professor, Department of World Missions Moody Bible Institute

With so many people still beyond the influence of a local church, we need a fresh look at the Great Commission passages. By revealing the sequential nature of Jesus' instructions to his followers and addressing key issues related to those instructions, this book can renew a biblical passion for God's pursuit of the least reached. I recommend it to every follower of Jesus.

Dr. Warren Janzen
General Director of SEND International

Commissioned brings a laser-like focus to our eternal purpose for living. It is a readable book which is likely to motivate you to courageously reorganize the priorities of your life according to Christ's explicit plan for you as part of His church. With this done, there will be no regrets.

Dr. Ted Barnett
U.S. Director, Africa Inland Mission

I confess. I thought I would just be reviewing another Great Commission "sermonette" when I first received this manuscript. Not that I mind that, but what I discovered was a fully developed text on Biblical Missiology, from one whose life has been marked by commitment and obedience to the last and greatest of our Lord's instructions to His followers. Dr. Newell has given us one of the most coherent, complete, and comprehensible overviews of our mission responsibility that I have seen. Furthermore, he has kept the main thing the main thing - evangelizing the entire world!

Dr. J. Ray Tallman
Professor and Chair of World Missions,
Golden Gate Baptist Theological Seminary
Mill Valley, CA

Commissioned

What Jesus Wants You to Know as You Go

By Marvin J. Newell

Published by ChurchSmart Resources

We are an evangelical Christian publisher committed to producing excellent products
at affordable prices to help church leaders accomplish effective ministry in the areas of
Church planting, Church growth, Church renewal and Leadership development.

All Scripture quotations in this book are taken from the English Standard Version (ESV)
copyrighted in 2001 by CrossWay Books.

For a free catalog of our resources call 1-800-253-4276.
Visit us at: www.ChurchSmart.com

Cover design by: Julie Becker
© Copyright 2010 by Marvin J. Newell

ISBN-10: 1-889638-89-7
ISBN-13: 978-1-889638-89-8

DEDICATION

This book is dedicated to my parents
Everitt and Ruby Newell
who first taught me the importance of
the Great Commission
and enthusiastically supported in every way
my participation in it.

Table of Contents

Foreword 11

Preface 15

Part 1: The Great Commission Passages 19

Chapter 1:
    Parting Words – Pressing Matters 21
Chapter 2:
    The Model for Mission 29
Chapter 3:
    The Magnitude of the Mission 39
Chapter 4:
    The Methodology for Mission 51
Chapter 5:
    The Message of Mission 67
Chapter 6:
    The Means of Mission 77

Part 2: Issues related to the Great Commission 89

Prologue to Part 2 91
Chapter 7:
    The Great Commission Diamond 93
Chapter 8:
    Common Questions About the Great Commission 111
Chapter 9:
    The Why of the Great Commission 125
Chapter 10:
    Leadership Principles from the Great Commission 137
Chapter 11:
    The Remaining Task 151
Chapter 12:
    The Great Commission and You 161

End Notes 167
Bibliography 177

Foreword

"Of the writing of books there is no end," says the old adage. To which I hasten to respond, "That's good – really good. Why? Because if there were an end to writing books it might have come before Marv Newell finished his new book *Commissioned: What Jesus Wants You to Know as You Go*. And that would have been bad – really bad!" Let me explain why.

Exactly 100 years ago in 1910, mission leaders convened a missionary conference generally reputed to be the most significant one up to that time – the World Missionary Conference in Edinburgh, Scotland. For all that was good about that conference, one aspect was just plain bad. Namely, in order to avoid possible disputes and divisions, organizers decided to disallow any and all theological and doctrinal discussions from the conference agenda. That decision resulted in the exclusion, not only of such doctrines as the inspiration of Scripture and the blood atonement, it also excluded discussion on the meaning of the Great Commission, and the very nature of Christian mission itself! Churches and missions were free to decide these matters for themselves quite apart from any external standard including the biblical text. I call their decision the "Edinburgh Error."

The "Edinburgh Error" was crucial because it set a precedent for future deliberations of the International Missionary Council and the ecumenical missionary movement of the 20th century. Mission and Commission were discussed in subsequent meetings to be sure. But there was no agreed upon commitment to the complete authority of the biblical text. As a result, the Great Commission came to be interpreted – and mission came to be defined – in accordance with prevailing interests: "The mission is church," "The church is mission," "The mission is *missio Dei*, the mission of God," "The mission is humanization," "Mission is what the church does in the world," "The mission is everything the church is sent to do in the world," "The mission is to preach good news to the poor," "The mission is to build the kingdom and establish shalom;" and so on.

In addition to contributing to confusion as to the nature of mission, the Edinburgh Error contributed to the virtual demise of world missions in the great conciliar denominations in North America. At the beginning of the 20th century those denominations supplied 80 percent of the North American missionary force. At its end, they supplied no more than six percent of it!

Happily, that is only part of the story. Theologically conservative leaders of the so-called "faith missions" soon responded to the Edinburgh Error and the inroads of liberalism in mainline churches and missions. In 1917 they formed the Interdenominational Foreign Mission Association (IFMA, now CrossGlobal Link) on the basis of a carefully crafted statement of faith. In the first article they affirmed the verbal inspiration, inerrancy (of the original manuscripts), infallibility and authority of the Bible as the Word of God. In subsequent articles they affirmed the historic doctrines of the Christian faith. Then, much later in the 1940s, denominational evangelical mission leaders took a cue from the IFMA and formed the Evangelical Fellowship of Mission Agencies (EFMA, now The Mission Exchange) on the basis of a very similar statement of faith.

Since the middle of the 20th century – and especially since the 1970s – conservative mission theorists of Pentecostal, fundamentalist and evangelical persuasions have developed a vast array of mission methods and strategies, and have pioneered missionary efforts of all kinds. All are well intentioned, of course, but all are not of equal value. In fact, some proposals entail interpretations of the Great Commission and understandings of Christian mission that are highly suspect.

In some respects, therefore, conservative Christians and mission leaders today face much the same challenge as did their liberal counterparts back in 1910. There is, however, one all-important difference. Thanks to the faithful precedent set by the founders of the IFMA and their successors, Pentecostal, fundamentalist and evangelical Christians today confess faith not only in the person of Christ, but also in the authority of Scripture and the truth of the gospel!

Now, after the passage of almost one hundred years, the IFMA/CrossGlobal Link has placed us in its debt yet again. Building on what he calls the "bedrock of Christian mission," CrossGlobal Link executive director Marv Newell has blessed us with another and fresh look at the "marching orders" of the Christian church – the Great Commission. His book could not be more timely. I cannot improve upon Newell's way of saying it:

> Today, when many distracting voices are calling believers
> to do good acts globally and call it 'mission,' when competing
> agendas to world evangelization suck the vigor and vitality
> out of its evangelistic fervor, and when those instructions of
> Jesus are being down-graded in favor of a more obscure and
> unexacting mandate, it behooves us to look again at what Jesus
> really told his followers they should be doing as they are going.

Finally, I have a word for anyone who may glance at this book and be tempted to respond, "Ho-hum, another book on the Great Commission. Who needs it?" To any such person I would like to say: This is not a ho-hum book by any means and all Christian believers – leaders and laypersons – need it! To be sure, its theme is as old as the church. But its treatment is fresh and as up-to-date as tomorrow.

In Part 1, Newell painstakingly places the various Great Commission commands in their chronological contexts and exegetes their complementary significances in a most masterful and meaningful way. Then, in Part 2, he deals with some of the most pressing missiological issues of our time and shows how a thorough application of Great Commission teaching not only informs them but also resolves them in ways that contribute to the fulfillment of the Great Commission.

With a view to the future of Christian mission in this 21st century, and especially now when we commemorate the World Missionary Conference at Edinburgh in 1910, this book should be number one on the reading list of true Christians everywhere. Buy it; read it; study it. And then loan it to a friend or two so they can study it too. Be sure that you loan it to friends who will return it, however. This is the kind of book you will want to have at arm's reach so you can refer to it again and again. This is the kind of book all of us will need to re-inform and re-invigorate Great Commission mission in the challenging days just ahead. Thank you Dr. Newell and CrossGlobal Link!

David J. Hesselgrave, Ph.D.
Professor Emeritus of Mission
Trinity Evangelical Divinity School
Deerfield, Illinois

Preface

C hristians today know it best as "The Great Commission," a label that has been around for nearly 500 years.[1] I routinely ask groups of believers if they know where in Scripture the Great Commission is found. Most correctly respond by saying, "Matthew 28," but are hard pressed to cite the exact verses. Acts 1:8 invariably comes in second. Sometimes, some mention that they know there must be another passage in the Gospels, but have difficulty nailing one down. Mark 16:15 sometimes squeaks through.

Maybe this is where you find yourself too. Most likely you know that Jesus instructed those who believe in him to share the good news of the gospel with others. Possibly you also understand that this good news message is so important that it needs to be heralded not only within your community, but also across countries, continents and into cultures wherever man is found. But even if this is where you are, you may have lingering questions as to exactly what Jesus intended regarding the *how* and the *why* of transmitting that message.

Unquestionably, the message, meaning, and importance of Jesus' "commission" to his followers has become increasingly difficult for the average believer to pinpoint. This difficulty is understandable when you stop to think about it.

Some find it difficult because they have never been shown from Scripture that in his post-resurrection days leading to his ascension into heaven, Jesus took great pains to explain to his disciples the details of what the next stage in redemptive history was to be in his absence – the spreading of his message of redemption to the entire world.

Others would know that the commission passages are multiple, but they mistakenly think the passages are synoptic rather than sequential, and thus miss the progressive nature of information Jesus relayed to his disciples. Still others understand that the commission passages are multiple and somewhat successive, but have failed to discover the threads running through them that detail how it is to be carried out. Finally, some question if it is even relevant for today.

This book is written to help followers of Christ understand just what Jesus intends for them to do as they go on mission for him! By taking a fresh look at the five "Great Commission" passages, the Commission's substance, scope, strategy and importance in God's redemptive plan become remarkably clear. Also, its relevance for the Church today becomes unquestionable.

Certainly the term "Great Commission" is familiar to most Christ-followers, but its instruction is not necessarily understood. *It is not that believers don't know about it; it's that many don't know how to go about it.* This book is intended to help believers do just that – to rediscover what Jesus, the author of the Great Commission, said they are to know as they go.

What is a "commission?"

The word "commission" is used in a variety of ways in the English language. A look at the typical dictionary definition of the word reveals its diverse meaning. Commission can mean the fee that is paid to an agent for providing a service. It can refer to a government agency or to a group of people authorized to carry out a task. It can indicate the appointment of a person to a rank in the armed forces. It can also mean to bring a ship into active service, or a facility into operation. All show the rich usage of the word in our language, but none of those describe what Jesus intended.[2]

The definition that best approximates what Jesus meant in reference to his commission is: "a task given to an individual or group, especially in order to produce a particular product or piece of work."[3] With this definition in hand, throughout this book "Great Commission" will mean:

> The task given by Jesus to the Church through the disciples that authorizes it to carry the gospel everywhere so that all peoples might have opportunity to believe on Christ as their Savior and become life-long followers of him.

We will discover that all five of the Great Commission passages have this intent at their core, though each present a particular emphasis.

Is there a paradox?

It needs to be mentioned that in the thinking of some there is an apparent paradox when it comes to understanding the importance of the Great Commission passages. On the one hand, if these passages never existed – if the resurrected Christ had never uttered them – there would still be indisputable grounds from many other New Testament passages that call believers to engage in world evangelization.

The Apostolic Church did not have the benefit of these passages. At least they did not have them in written form from which to draw upon as justification for their evangelistic zeal. For the first thirty years, up into the early AD 60's, these words of Jesus had not been written down.[4] Nonetheless that period was one of the most prolific evangelistic eras in all Church history!

On the other hand, as Herbert Kane rightly observed, "There are many reasons why the church should engage in world evangelization, but the paramount reason is the command of Christ."[5] John Stott adds, "We engage in evangelism today not because we want to, or because we choose to or because we like to, but because we have been told to. The Church is under orders. The risen Lord has commanded us to 'go' to 'preach,' to 'make disciples' and that is enough for us."[6]

The bedrock of Christian mission

The idea of going on mission to propagate the gospel is not peripheral to the New Testament. Jesus commanded the church to "go" primarily through his five Great Commission statements, which serve as the Divine Charter for global outreach. These passages constitute the very bedrock of the Christian mission. Some go so far as to say that the Gospels culminate in the Great Commission as the real center of the New Testament, to which everything after them leads onward.[7] Whether or not this is the case, these passages do function as the hinge between the four Gospels and the rest of the New Testament, making sense of what follows.

The Great Commission passages contain the missional mandate for the entire Church, commanding it to be a universally witnessing community. This mandate was not hatched at a gathering of zealous deacons in the back of a church who had nothing else to do on a lazy Sunday afternoon! No, the mandate was given to the Church by none other than the Savior of the world himself. Why? Because he wanted to ensure that knowledge of his costly provision for salvation would not go unnoticed. Nor did he want the call for a right relationship with God to go unheeded. He wanted it to reach all mankind.

It is left to us then, to look at these mission statements Jesus carefully crafted, to come to a fuller understanding of how genuine mission is to be conducted. To use a military metaphor, the Commander-in-Chief himself gave the marching orders to the Church. His orders, found in his five mission statements, are clear, precise, logically set forth and masterfully crafted.

> The concern for world evangelization is not something tacked on to a man's personal Christianity, which he may take or leave as he chooses. It is rooted in the character of the God who has come to us in Christ Jesus. Thus, it can never be the province of a few enthusiasts, a sideline or a specialty of those who happen to have a bent that way. It is the distinctive mark of being a Christian.
>
> – James S. Stewart

Why this fresh look at the Great Commission?

Today, when many distracting voices are calling believers to do good acts globally and call it "mission," when competing agendas to world evangelization suck the vigor and vitality out of its evangelistic fervor,[8] and when these instructions of Jesus are being downgraded in favor of a more obscure and unexacting mandate,[9] it behooves us to look again at what Jesus really told his followers they are to be doing as they are going.

The best place to start down the road to Great Commission familiarity is to identify where these passages are located. Then the settings in which they were given need to be understood. Finally, we need to piece them together in the chronological order in which Jesus gave them to his disciples.

PART 1

Chapter 1

Parting Words – Pressing Matters

Final words of a departing loved one are always taken seriously. This is especially true if that person is saying farewell for the very last time. When those words contain instruction about a pressing and dear matter, the departing one will take extraordinary measures to convey them. It is not unusual for those words to be profound and even provocative. They are usually well thought out and masterfully crafted beforehand. Often they are written in a "last will and testament" to assure they will be accurately carried out once the person has passed on.

In the days following his resurrection, Jesus met with his disciples on several different occasions. You'll recall reading in the Gospels about him meeting them in a room in Jerusalem, on a mountainside in Galilee, by the Sea of Galilee, and on the slopes of the Mount of Olives. He met with his disciples at several different times and in a variety of places in order that he might impart to them final instructions that were crucially important to him.

To be sure, during his post-resurrection appearances Jesus passed along other information to his disciples as well. But his final days with them were bookended with instruction about the upcoming worldwide mission they were to inaugurate. He first told them about it on the evening of Resurrection Day. He last instructed them in it 40 days later, just moments before victoriously ascending into heaven.

Throughout history these passages have been given various labels. The most common has been "commission." This word is found in most Bibles imbedded somewhere in Matthew chapter 28 with the adjective "great" modifying it. Another term that has been used to emphasize the importance of these passages has been "mandate." Some have said these passages comprise the "marching orders" for the church. Others have called them "the divine charter" of Christian missions."[1] No matter what the preferred nomenclature, the importance of these passages – revealing the outward missional responsibility of the church – cannot be missed.

The Great Commission passages

The final chapter of each Gospel (final two of John) along with the first chapter of Acts record Jesus' final discourses to the disciples. Within these chapters we discover what has come to be known as his five "Great Commission" mission statements. If one were to read them in order, they would appear as follows:

Matthew 28:18-20
> [18] And Jesus came and said to them, "All authority in heaven and on earth has been given to me. [19] Go therefore and make disciples of all nations, baptizing them in the name of the Father and of the Son and of the Holy Spirit, [20] teaching them to observe all that I have commanded you. And behold, I am with you always, to the end of the age."

Mark 16:15
> And he said to them, "Go into all the world and proclaim the gospel to the whole creation."

Luke 24:44-49
> [44] Then he said to them, "These are my words that I spoke to you while I was still with you, that everything written about me in the Law of Moses and the Prophets and the Psalms must be fulfilled." [45] Then he opened their minds to understand the Scriptures, [46] and said to them, "Thus it is written that the Christ should suffer and on the third day rise from the dead, [47] and that repentance and forgiveness of sins should be proclaimed in his name to all nations, beginning from Jerusalem. [48] You are witnesses of these things. [49] And behold, I am sending the promise of my Father upon you. But stay in the city until you are clothed with power from on high."

John 20:21

> Jesus said to them again, "Peace be with you. As the Father has sent me, even so I am sending you."

Acts 1:8

> "But you will receive power when the Holy Spirit has come upon you, and you will be my witnesses in Jerusalem and in all Judea and Samaria, and to the end of the earth."

Putting them in chronological order

One of the most common mistakes made when reading through the Gospels is to treat these passages as though they were synoptic. "Synoptic" means to view as the same, or to put it differently, to see these passages as given at one time, conveying the same thought but from different angles. Many harmonies of the Gospels misleadingly construct them as such.

However, a closer look at the context surrounding these passages reveals otherwise. Upon examination of the contexts and settings where Jesus conveyed them, it becomes apparent that Jesus gave these mission statements to his disciples on five different occasions, in five different addresses, at five different geographical settings, with five different emphases.

That being the case, it becomes evident that these statements are sequential rather than synoptic. Chronologically, Jesus gave them in an order much different from the biblical order in which one finds them if read starting with Matthew. As was already mentioned, noting the contexts surrounding these passages reveals the true order in which he gave them.

On the evening of resurrection day, Jesus met with ten distraught disciples in a room in Jerusalem (Jn. 20:19). For reasons we do not know, Thomas was absent from this first meeting and Judas was dead, leaving only ten disciples present. At that meeting Jesus gave the briefest of the commissions, as found in John 20:21.

Eight days later (Jn. 20:26), when Thomas was present, Jesus gave to the eleven disciples the added information of Mark 16:15. About a week or so following that, he met with the disciples a third time, after they had walked all the way to Galilee to meet with him there. It was there that Jesus gave the most detailed of the commissions, recorded in Matthew 28:18-20.

Approximately two weeks after that, on the eve of his ascension after the disciples had walked back to Jerusalem, Jesus gave the Luke 24:44-49 commission.[2] Finally, possibly after an interval of only a few short hours, Jesus gave his farewell mission statement recorded by Luke in Acts 1:8.

Thus, the chronological order in which Jesus gave the "Great Commission" would be:

John 20:21
      Mark 16:15
            Matthew 28:18-20
                    Luke 24:44-49
                          Acts 1:8

Resurrection   40 days   Ascension

Why this order?

Why would Jesus have given the Great Commission to the disciples in this order? Remembering the tension of those days and fragile emotional state of the disciples, there are several considerations that help make sense of this number and order:

1) He wanted to incrementally impart to the disciples information about their next mission, so they could adequately grasp and comprehend it. Incremental information, the process of adding a little more detail at each successive setting, allowed the disciples time to slowly digest the essence of what Jesus was conveying to them. This was to be a lifelong task in which they were being asked to engage. It would have global significance. They needed to get it right.

During their three years with him, Jesus had the disciples periodically engage in restrictive outreaches. Those outreaches were limited in time, scope and message. However, all that was going to change now. A greater mission awaited them. By conveying his instructions in incremental stages, Jesus was giving them time to decipher and comprehend the magnitude of the task he was leaving them.

2) The disciples were in no frame of mind to absorb in one sitting the full measure of instruction he was passing along to them. The recent events of Jesus' trials, death and resurrection had left them traumatized! They were in a state of uncertainty and confusion. They were in no condition to comprehend the details of this new assignment. Therefore, Jesus wisely spoon-fed the information to them, in bite size portions as it were, so they would be capable of digesting it.

3) By teaching through repetition, Jesus was emphasizing its importance. He was showing them how crucial their new task really was to the plan of redemption. Just as a parent warns or instructs a child several times about an important matter so that the seriousness of it is captured, so too Jesus employed this pedagogical method to impress upon the disciples the importance of their next task.

The following chart demonstrates the progressive and incremental elements of the Great Commission statements:

Passage	Location	When	To Whom	Mandate	Emphasis
John 20:21	Jerusalem	Evening of resurrection day	10 disciples	"As the Father has sent me ..."	The Model
Mark 16:15	Jerusalem	8 days later	11 disciples	"go into all the world ... to the whole creation."	The Magnitude
Matthew 28:18-20	Mountain in Galilee	Between 1-2 weeks later	11 disciples	"... make disciples of all nations ..."	The Method
Luke 24:44-49	Jerusalem	About 40 days after the resurrection	11 disciples	"... repentance and forgiveness of sins ..."	The Message
Acts 1:8	Mount of Olives	40 days after the resurrection	11 disciples	"you will receive power ... Jerusalem, Judea, Samaria ..."	The Means

So, it is clear that Jesus did not give the Great Commission to the disciples all at once. This was too important a task to be handled so quickly. There was too great a chance for misunderstanding. There was too much detail to be absorbed. There was the risk that it would not have become a priority to them and consequently they would never have done it. For the sake of clarity, Jesus had to give it over and over and over again.

Relation between the Great Commission and personal commissions

Are there other Great Commission passages in Scripture other than the four found in the Gospels and the one in the Book of Acts? No, there are not. Nevertheless we do know of other divinely given personal commissions to individual messengers in New Testament times. However, none of them were addressed to the whole church, nor concerned the whole mission to the whole world. Instead, they were limited in either time, scope or to the individual's personal involvement. It is clear that each of them perfectly aligned with the overriding mandates found in the Great Commission passages.

The book of Acts presents us with some excellent examples of personal commissions. Philip was given a commission to go evangelize an influential Ethiopian (Acts 8: 26), Ananias of Damascus was commissioned to reach out to Saul (Acts 9:10-15), Peter was commissioned to go meet Cornelius' household (Acts 10:19-20), and Paul was given a commission to evangelize Gentiles (Acts 26:17-18). While the others were time-limited assignments, Paul's was a commission for life.

It is this personal commission to Paul that is the most intriguing. Although given directly from Jesus to him at the time of his conversion, it wasn't until 25 years later that Paul reveals its content. And instead of telling the churches about it (at least in writing), we find it in Acts 26 as part of his legal defense before King Agrippa. Here in his own words is what he said:

> [14] And when we had all fallen to the ground, I heard a voice saying to me in the Hebrew language, 'Saul, Saul, why are you persecuting me? It is hard for you to kick against the goads.' [15] And I said, 'Who are you, Lord?' And the Lord said, 'I am Jesus whom you are persecuting. [16] But rise and stand upon your feet, for I have appeared to you for this purpose, to appoint you as a servant and witness to the things in which you have seen me and to those in which I will appear to you, [17] delivering you from your people and from the Gentiles – to whom I am sending you [18] to open their eyes, so that they may turn from darkness to light and from the power of Satan to God, that they may receive forgiveness of sins and a place among those who are sanctified by faith in me.'

This is one of the most beautiful and exacting commissions ever given to an individual – one every missionary could wish to have. Jesus told Paul that he was sending him out as a pioneer missionary. Included in Paul's commission are some basic elements:

1. The Sender: "I am Jesus whom you are persecuting….I am sending…"
2. The sent one: " Saul, Saul…I am sending you…"
3. Those to whom he is sent, "…the Gentiles…"
4. His assignment: "…to open their eyes, so that they may turn from darkness to light and from the power of Satan to God, that they may receive forgiveness of sins and a place among those who are sanctified by faith in me."

Is this a genuine missionary commission? Absolutely. Is it on par with the Great Commission passages? No it is not. It has built-in limitations, whereas the Great Commission does not. Paul's was personal and not intended to be universally obeyed by every believer.

So it is with other personal commissions or "missionary callings" that Jesus loves giving to willing and receptive hearts. Perhaps you have experienced one yourself. These can be direct, jolting, passionate and unquestionably clear. Yet none of them – not even Paul's – are to be placed on par with the Great Commission. The combined Great Commission passages are the "mother ship" commission addressed to the whole Church. Out of them, all personal commissions or "missionary calls" (as they are commonly referred to) are launched, and so, consequently, tethered to them.

What becomes fascinating when spending time in these passages is to discover how they contain all the essential ingredients necessary for successful mission. This holds true for the church in any age wherever and whenever it does mission.

> ➢ In chapter 2 we will discover the *Model* for doing mission from the greatest missionary who ever graced this planet – Jesus himself.
> ➢ In chapter 3 we will delve into the *Magnitude* of the task of missions. By it we will see how much more of the task still remains to be completed.
> ➢ Chapter 4 deals with the most recognized Great Commission passage of all – Matthew 28:18-20. From it we discover the *Methodology* Jesus wants us to employ even as we do mission today.

➢ Every mission intends to communicate something deemed important. In chapter 5 we will see precisely what *Message* Jesus wants proclaimed to all peoples everywhere.

➢ Chapter 6 examines the three important *Means* of mission – empowerment, the strategic plan for expansion, and human instrumentality.

Other related issues are dealt with in part two of this book, but it is these first six chapters that deal in depth with the Great Commission mission statements of Jesus.

What Jesus wants you to know as you go...

The Great Commission passages are the parting words of Jesus. By them he forthrightly addresses the pressing matter of spreading his Good News to the nations. This is something the disciples were to inaugurate. It was something they were to be doing after he departed.

Methodically, one-by-one, Jesus relayed to them the essence of the Great Commission. He met with them at five different times in five different settings to give them five different components of his mission. He passed these along to them incrementally so they would be able to grasp the progression and importance of this teaching.

Jesus would subsequently give other personal commissions to other followers as well. But each of them would be tied to, and fall in line with, the five mission addresses given to the disciples. Without question these five mission statements of Jesus make up the missional Magna Carta of the Church, from its inception, for today, and into the future.

Chapter 2

The Model for Mission

Over and over again throughout history God has shown himself to be a missionary God. As such he has little problem sending anyone, anywhere at anytime. For the benefit of his plans and purposes, he sends people from where they are to where he needs them so that his divine will might be accomplished and his name most glorified.

Scriptures abound with stories of God sending people on mission. Whenever he had an important task to accomplish, he sent someone to get it done. He sent Noah and his family into the ark to save mankind from the flood. He sent Abraham from Ur to the land of Palestine. He sent Jacob to Haran and back to preserve the Jewish bloodline. He sent Joseph into Egypt; Moses from the desert of Midian to the court of Pharaoh; the Israelites out of Egypt; Daniel to Babylon; and Jonah to Nineveh, to name a few.

Then, when it came time to fulfill his redemptive plan, he sent his Son, Jesus, from heaven to earth; the wise men to Bethlehem; and Joseph and Mary to Egypt and back. Some years later he sent John the Baptist to prepare the way for Jesus' public ministry. After Jesus' ministry was complete, God sent the Holy Spirit to the church, and then the church into all the world.

As part of that process to transmit the good news of redemption throughout the world, Jesus sent out the disciples by way of his Great Commission statements. His people have been on mission ever since. The living God is indeed a missionary God![1]

What does it mean to be sent on mission? Whether a diplomatic, business or religious mission, the term *mission* presupposes four necessary components. Every mission entails 1) a sender, 2) the one sent, 3) those to whom one is sent, and 4) an assignment. The entire process presumes that the one doing the sending has the authority to do so.[2]

We read something fascinating at the end of each Gospel that the disciples had not anticipated. They hadn't a clue of what Jesus was going to ask of them next. They hadn't a clue that Jesus was going to send them on a global mission that would be picked up and carried on by all believers who came after them. So his first order of business was to make contact with them.

Jesus meets the disciples

Following Jesus' crucifixion, the disciples hid themselves in a room somewhere in Jerusalem. It was dangerous for them, his followers, to be out and about on the streets. The room they were hiding in could well have been the same room in which they had celebrated the Passover with Jesus just days earlier. Whether or not it was, Jesus knew where they were and made a jaw-dropping appearance. He suddenly appeared unannounced in their midst, even though they were secured behind closed doors (John 20:19).

Jesus wasted no time telling them of their next assignment. The first hint to the disciples that he wanted them to engage in a global-wide endeavor that would take them out of the confines of Israel, took place that evening – the same day of his resurrection. In this first post-resurrection meeting with them, he mentioned the bare essence of their new assignment. His words were brief to be sure, but enough was said to get them thinking about what they were to do next. John records Jesus' words as follows:

> Jesus said to them again, "Peace be with you. As the Father has sent me, even so I am sending you." John 20:21

Have you ever noticed what Jesus did not include in this brief commission? He did not tell them where they were to go, how far they were to go, how long they were to go, why they were to go, nor the specifics of the message they were to take with them. Instead, his objective at this point was simply to inform them that they were being sent to do something different from what they had ever done in the past.

Peace and mission

However, before Jesus could even begin to hint to the disciples that he had a new plan for them, he first had to set their minds at ease. They had gathered that evening behind closed doors fearful their enemies might discover them! As followers of a recently condemned criminal, they had good reason to fear for their lives. If their leader could be unjustly tried and quickly executed, so could they. It was dangerous for them to be identified by anyone outside their tiny circle.

Once they had gathered together, they marveled at strange messages received throughout the day from several individuals claiming that Jesus had been seen alive. It was while they were discussing the validity of those reports that Jesus appears in their midst and shows himself to them.

Jesus knew that this would be a difficult teachable moment. In their present state of mind the disciples were not prepared to process the mind-boggling reports they had heard about Jesus, let alone accept new teaching from him. These bewildered men were mentally and emotionally exhausted. They were broken-hearted, disappointed and directionless all at the same time. With their leader unexpectedly killed, their plans had been shattered and their dreams of future greatness destroyed. They had lost everything – or at least they supposed. In the midst of this frame of mind Jesus stands among them and calmly says:

"Peace be with you."

Jesus was well aware that his first task was to restore their mental and emotional equilibrium. He probably spoke even more words of reassurance to them than John recorded, but these are the ones that stood out when he wrote his Gospel decades later. These words of reassurance and confidence were just what the disciples needed at this time of confusion. Once calmed, they were prepared to hear what Jesus had to say next.

There is an important lesson for us today in these words. These words of calm and peace are as heartening to Christ-followers and missionaries in this age as they were to the disciples back then. In a world full of uncertainty, messengers of Christ are to possess the peace of Christ, for their very task is to present to the world the Prince of Peace. Those who have experienced peace with God also have peace within themselves. Inner peace of a pardoned sinner grounds the heart for service and witness even in the midst of external turmoil.

Jesus sends the disciples

Once calm and peace had been established, Jesus adds the words:

"As the Father has sent me, even so I am sending you."

This new initiative, a foreign thrust of going outside of Israel, was a seismic change in the way God would now utilize his Chosen People in relation to other nations. In Old Testament times Israel functioned primarily as a magnet, drawing nations to the light of God through their life experience with him. That drawing is referred to as "centripetal mission" whereby Israel, on the strength of their exemplary reputation and obedience to God, drew peoples of other nations to Jerusalem, to the temple, and ultimately to God.[3] Passages such as Isaiah 60:1-3 were embedded in the minds of the disciples:

Arise, shine, for your light has come, and the glory of the Lord rises upon you. See, darkness covers the earth and thick darkness is over the peoples, but the Lord rises upon you and his glory appears over you. Nations will come to your light, and kings to the brightness of your dawn.

Now, Jesus is telling his disciples that the plan was dramatically changed. The missional plan would now be just the opposite. Instead of centering their witness in Jerusalem and waiting for the nations to be drawn to them, they were to leave Jerusalem and fan out across the Roman Empire and beyond on a centrifugal, outward mission. This thrusting forth from Jerusalem constituted a huge reversal of tactics; and the disciples understood it. They realized they were being asked to do mission the opposite way of what they had known and seen practiced.

Sent to send

It is without question that the Father sent Jesus to earth on a mission. Twenty-nine times in the Gospel of John Jesus says that he was here on earth because God had sent him. He knew he was here on mission.

Without getting overly technical it is helpful to understand the words behind "send" in John 20:21. There are two different words for "send" in Greek, and Jesus uses both in this verse. One, *apostello*, carries the idea of a person being officially sent on a mission which has unquestionable authorization behind it. When defending his authority, Jesus uses this word fifteen different times in the dialogues found in the Gospel of John to relate God's sending of himself.

The other word, *pempo*, does not carry so much the meaning of an "official delegate" or "authorized sent one." It has more to do with the sending process – like when one clicks the "send" button on an email message. In the Gospel of John, Jesus uses this word twenty-four different times in reference to himself being sent by the Father. His choice of the words depended upon the emphasis he was making.

However, there are times when both words are found coupled together in the same sentence. When they are, the force of the authorized mission (*apostello*) is imposed on the second word (*pempo*). John 7:28-29 is a good example. This coupled usage of the two words is how Jesus purposefully expressed his commission in John 20:21. The verse literally reads,

> "As the father has officially sent me on an authorized mission (*apostello*),
> even so I am sending (*pimpo*) you out."

In other words, Jesus wanted his disciples to clearly understand that he was now propelling them forth – like an instantly released email, but at the same level of authorization by which he himself had been sent. By using these two words, the right to go forward was not lost on the disciples. Christ does not merely leave his disciples in the world, he sends them into it. Jesus was not only giving them authority to go, but the followers after them would keep on going as well.[4]

Three transmissions – same authority

As mentioned earlier, the sending on any kind of a mission, whether diplomatic, business, or religious presumes that the one doing the sending has the authority to do so. John 20:21 reveals where the authority for the sending of believers originates. It starts with God the Father who, as creator of the universe, has the sovereign right to send.

The authority behind the Great Commission starts and ends with Almighty God. It has its origin in God the Father. It is transmitted to the disciples through Jesus the Son, and is vicariously passed on by the disciples through the Spirit to believers in each subsequent generation.

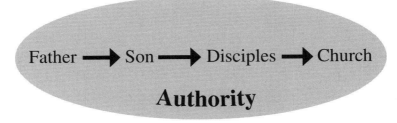

Father ➤ Son ➤ Disciples ➤ Church
Authority

This mandate to the Church did not originate in any church council, by papal edict, or at an ecclesiastical assembly. The mission of the Church originated in the eternal will of God the Father, proceeded through the historical mission of the Son in the world, was passed along to the disciples, and subsequently flows to every generation of believers by the presence of the Holy Spirit. Our mission is ongoing and grounded in divine authority.

Modeling the way

An important trait of an effective leader is that he be a model in life and practice to those who know him. An effective leader models the ideals he desires his followers to emulate. By his conduct he establishes the standard by which constituents, peers, and colleagues are expected to follow suit. By example he also establishes the pace and manner in which organizational goals are pursued. Through modeling the way, a leader sets the bar of excellence others are expected to reach.[5]

Jesus, by way of his life and ministry, set the standard for how his followers are to conduct themselves while engaged in the task of carrying the gospel to the world. His life became the impeccable model for everything: character, morals, ethical behavior and performance. By emulating his life, no follower of Jesus will ever need to question whether his conduct is consistent with the gospel he proclaims. Nor will he ever be put to shame.

A word of caution is important if one is determined to perfectly duplicate the ministry of Jesus and not just his character. Although some say it is incumbent on Jesus' messengers to seamlessly define their ministry by his example, this can never be achieved. Jesus is an impossible model to exactly replicate! No person today can declare or define his or her ministry as Jesus did his in Luke 4:18-19: "proclaiming freedom for prisoners and recovery of sight for the blind, to release the oppressed, to proclaim the year of the Lord's favor."[6] Only he could do those sorts of things (a more detailed discussion of this is found in chapter 8).

Therefore, because of Jesus' unique personhood and mission, the disciples could not perfectly model their ministries after his. Neither can we. Stop and think for a moment about Jesus' unique salvific mission: 1) he was born to die for the sins of the world (Lk. 19:10); 2) confined his mission to the Jewish people (Mt.10:6); and 3) performed unique miraculous "signs" and "wonders" that were meant to authenticate and separate his mission from all others (Jn. 2:11; 4:54; 7:31).[7]

How could one begin to think that he or she could or should match that? There is a huge distinction between the mission of Jesus with that which is ours. If we don't recognize this, we are doomed to deviate from what Jesus really would have us do. Some go so far as to say that those who do not distinguish the work of Jesus from that which he gave to his disciples cannot be credible.[8]

This whole discussion begs the next logical question. If Christ-followers are unable to copy Jesus in what was his unique mission to the world, then in what way are they to emulate him? The answer is found in the humanity of Jesus. Jesus models the way for his ambassadors through his human attributes. The life of Jesus as a person is the same life to be lived out by all Christ-followers.

It is possible then to look to Jesus as the prototype missionary that the rest of us should follow.[9] Following his lead in matters pertaining to his humanity should be every worker's goal.

"As...so"

In John 20:21 the two conjunctions "As...so" show by comparison how one can follow Jesus' model in personal conduct and public ministry. The word "as" (*kathos*) means "in like manner." The solemn teaching of Jesus is that his messengers are to manifest his life and character "in like manner" in their ministries as well. Just as Jesus manifested godly character in the world, believers are to bear that same kind of witness in life as they minister.

Using the comparison "As the Father ... so I am sending you," consider fourteen statements Jesus made about himself during his lifetime that we as his messengers should model in our personal mission.

As to:

Mission: "For the Son of Man came to seek and to save the lost." (Lk. 19:10)
                                                            "...so I am sending you."

Motivation: "I work for the honor of the One who sent me." (Jn. 7:18 paraphrased)
                                                            "...so I am sending you."

Objective: "I came that they may have life and have it abundantly." (Jn. 10:10)
                                                            "...so I am sending you."

Offer: "Come to me, all who labor and are heavy laden, and I will give you rest." (Mt. 11:28)

"…so I am sending you."

Focus: "I came not to call the righteous, but sinners (to repentance)." (Mt. 9:13)

"…so I am sending you."

Will: "My food is to do the will of him who sent me and to accomplish his work." (Jn. 4:34)

"…so I am sending you."

Relationships: "The Son of Man has come…as a friend of tax collectors and sinners." (Lk.7:34)

"…so I am sending you."

Teamwork: "And he appointed twelve so that they might be with him and he might send them out to preach." (Mark 3:14)

"…so I am sending you."

Servanthood: "…the Son of Man came not to be served but to serve …." (Mt. 20:28)

"…so I am sending you."

Personality: "…learn from me, for I am gentle and lowly in heart…" (Mt. 11:29)

"…so I am sending you."

Approval: "…I always do the things that are pleasing to him." (Jn. 8:29)

"…so I am sending you."

Ownership: "…the Son of Man has nowhere to lay his head." (Mt. 8:20)

"…so I am sending you."

Compassion: "When he saw the crowds, he had compassion for them, because they were harassed and helpless, like sheep without a shepherd." (Mt. 9:36)

"…so I am sending you."

Finishing well: "I glorified you on earth, having accomplished the work that you gave me to do." (Jn. 17:4).

"…so I am sending you."

The right to speak

Jesus deliberately made his mission the model of what ours ought to be. What he portrayed in life and practice his servants are to do as they go into the world. The model of Jesus is the rod by which all personal conduct and ministry activities are to be measured. We gain the right to speak based on the right life from which we speak. Our lifestyle is right if it is modeled after Christ's. It is then that his servants are deemed worthy to proclaim the gospel.

A.W. Tozer once said, "The first priority of the church is not to spread the gospel of Jesus Christ. The first priority of the church is to make it worthy to spread the gospel of Jesus Christ." That is why Count Nicholas Zinzendorf, the founder of the Moravians, one of the earliest and largest mission movements from Germany, could declare, "I have one passion, it is he, it is he alone!"

When a clothing designer wants to model her new apparel, she does it in one of two ways. One way is by putting the new designs on human-like mannequins for display. By this method people must go to a store to discover the new designs for themselves. Another way is for her to put her new designs on living models. The models then show them off by walking a central runway that extends right into the midst of an audience. Christ's ambassadors display his attributes by both methods. The conduct of those on mission can't be missed as they are constantly on display "walking the runway" among watching peoples.

What about holistic ministry?

There have been some who have used this short commission passage to claim that social concern is at the core of the church's mission. For that reason some have gravitated away from the other four more detailed Great Commission passages to elevate this one to a place of preeminence. They are compelled to do so because it seems for them that this is the only Great Commission passage that contains a hint of social responsibility attached to it – the social action model of Jesus.

Only by ignoring the other Great Commission passages and holding solely to this one found in John – the briefest and most vague of the five – can they justify their position.[10] Alarmingly, this is becoming an increasingly popular yet truncated interpretation of Jesus' Great Commission.

The point here is not to say that the church is free from any social responsibility or should not engage in holistic ministry as it goes on mission. There is plenty of evidence from the life and teaching of both Jesus and the apostles that shows that it should. Believers have both an evangelistic obligation as well as a moral obligation to help mankind whenever they engage in mission. However to elevate holistic ministry as a higher priority or even equal in importance to evangelistic ministry is difficult if not impossible to establish from this one passage. This issue is so important it will be dealt with in more detail in a separate discussion in chapter eight.

What Jesus wants you to know as you go...

In his first Great Commission statement to his disciples, Jesus focused on the very meaning of mission – that of being sent. God's design for reaching the nations is now being completely reversed. Up until now the nations were to go to Israel to discover God and his salvation. Now, starting with the disciples, the Church has the task of taking that knowledge to the world.

Jesus made it clear that the authority behind the mission is given from God Himself. This makes the right and the responsibility of engaging in mission unquestionable. How were they personally to engage in that mission? By following the ministry model set by Jesus himself.

Jesus gave this first commission to the disciples on resurrection night. From that time onward, the disciples knew things were to be different. Although details were sketchy, they realized they were being sent out to do something totally different from the past. They would "be turning the world upside down" (Acts 17:6).

The Building Blocks of the Great Commission

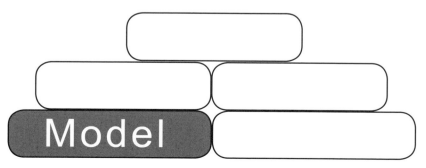

Chapter 3

The Magnitude of the Mission

J esus met with the disciples a second time in another surprise visit. It was eight days later at a rented room somewhere in Jerusalem. It may have been the same place as his first post-resurrection encounter with them the week before. The location isn't as important as what took place.

By comparing John 20:24-29 with Mark 16:15, we know Jesus had a couple of objectives for meeting with them this second time. One was to reassure Thomas, who had been absent from the previous meeting, that he really was alive and well. The other was to impart additional information to all eleven about the task ahead of them. There were only eleven disciples present as Judas the traitor did not survive the Passion Week events.

The disciples, having had a week to mull over their first encounter with Jesus, seem to have been as unprepared for this second encounter as they were for the first. The writer Mark states they were eating together when he appeared in their midst. Startled by his sudden entry through locked doors, Jesus immediately calmed their nerves by saying "peace be with you."

Just what had the disciples been discussing among themselves before Jesus' arrival? No doubt, besides the grandeur of the resurrection itself, the other hot topic must have been the implications to them personally of Jesus' announcement the previous week that they were now being sent somewhere else. But to where and to whom they were going had been left unclear; and equally puzzling was what exactly they were to do as they went.

So, at this second encounter, Jesus became more specific about the mission on which he was sending them. He knew that the emotional shock of his death, burial and resurrection was beginning to subside. They could now think more coherently. They were in a better state of mind to receive additional information. He used this time with them to convey two additional pieces of information: 1) the magnitude of the task ahead of them, and 2) the overall goal of their mission.

Into all the world

Once the disciples had calmed, Jesus revealed his wounds to a doubting Thomas. Thomas in return responded in belief (John 20:29). This special personal attention to Thomas was to become significant to world evangelization, as we will later see.

Jesus then turned his attention upon all eleven disciples, giving them the second installment of the Great Commission. The apostle Peter, who was the eyewitness source behind Mark's Gospel account, remembers Jesus' command as follows:

> "Go into all the world and proclaim the gospel to the whole creation."
> (Mk 16:15)

Jesus used two phrases that showed the disciples the largeness or magnitude of the task ahead of them: "into all the world" and "to the whole creation." Their minds must have reeled as they contemplated the enormity of the task! Jesus had said some challenging things to them in the past, but now their new mission was to include the entire world and the entire creation? How could that possibly be?

Jesus' use of the word "all" is significant. In seminary I recall a professor telling the class that when you encounter the word "all" in Scripture, be assured that "all means all and that's all all means." Jesus' inclusion of "all" was showing both an extent and a vast inclusiveness.

The word behind "all" of "all the world" is the word *hapas*, which is all-inclusive every time it is used. Jesus is making it clear to his disciples that they are to cover the entire earth with the gospel. Every part of the globe was to hear this good news. No continent was to be excluded, no geographical region ignored. No distance was to be considered too far and no people group too remote. The whole earth was to be covered with the message of Jesus' redemption – the good news, or "gospel." Their task was to be nothing short of global proportion!

To the whole creation

The second indication of the largeness of the task ahead of them was Jesus' command to reach the "whole creation." The word behind "whole" is the Greek word *pasa*, which more precisely translates "every, or each one." Some English versions more accurately translate it so.

The point Jesus is making to his disciples is that along with viewing the task as being geographically global, he also wants them to understand it in bite size portions and individually. People everywhere are to be presented with the gospel on a personal basis by ones, by families, or by groups. Just as "all the world" shows that the task is nothing short of global in extension, so "whole creation" shows the task as nothing short of an "each person" inclusion. Messengers of Christ are to have a zeal and priority for personal, one-to-one evangelism that reaches to every individual.

Some may ask why Jesus used the words " whole creation" instead of something like "all people," or "each person." Why does he include the full created order in the specific human need of redemption? The answer is not hard to discover. Not only is mankind affected by the fall, but all of creation as well. It too is in need of redemption (Romans 8:18-22) and reconciliation (Colossians 1:19-20). That does not mean we should be preaching to the hills and the trees, birds and animals, for the message is human specific.

However, creation itself is positively affected too! When fallen men are redeemed, their entire worldview changes. Instead of abusing creation, they become aware of making beneficial use of it. In turn, they put into place those practices that better the natural world around them. They become responsible stewards of God's creation. This becomes a natural collateral advantage and benefit in cultures when people align themselves aright with the Creator of all things. Instead of creation being misused it is redeemed through Christ's redemptive work as well.[1] So as people believe and receive the gospel, all of creation gets included in that redemption. The positive effects of human redemption spill over into the entire created order.

Going green

It is popular today for Christians to be involved in the "green" movement. Environmental quality and concerns seem to be on everyone's mind. To link those concerns with the Great Commission would help justify engaging in those green activities, making them a legitimate part of mission. So naturally the question is asked, does this verse include "eco-justice" as part of the Great Commission mandate?

The answer is yes and no, but more "no" than "yes." No, this is not a part of Christ's mandate by direct order, nor is it what Jesus was teaching here. It would be a stretch to suggest this is what Jesus had in mind when teaching his disciples only a week after paying the terrible penalty for man's sin. Mankind's redemption, not creation renewal, was at the core of this commission. Evangelization was the goal, not beautification. The groaning of mankind under the burden of sin (Romans 8:1-4) was the focus, not the groaning of creation under the burden of sinful man (Romans 8:19-22).[2]

However, although eco-justice is not a part of the church's mission by command, it is a natural by-product of the church's mission by application. The positive affects of human redemption have implications and application to the created world as well; they spill over positively into all of the created world. Through man's belief in Jesus, the world becomes a better, safer, cleaner place in which to live.

World evangelization

Besides telling his disciples the magnitude of their task in terms of its geographic expansiveness, Jesus took this opportunity to also tell them of the magnitude of their assignment in terms of what was to be the overall goal. Specifically, they were to "proclaim the gospel." This is a strongly specific and evangelistic phrase. However some are confused as to what it means. A closer examination of the phrase helps discover what Jesus intended.

> The gospel is only good news if it gets there in time.
> – Carl F. H. Henry

The word "proclaim" is the only imperative in this command of Jesus. Now, we shouldn't get the idea that Jesus was commanding each disciple and every follower after them to become seasoned preachers or expert pulpiteers. Rather Jesus is emphasizing the duty to outrightly proclaim the gospel. He wanted to ensure that they understood, just as we should today, that the message of redemption has to be vocalized to people. When these words "proclaim the gospel" are used together, most every time they could and should be translated with the singular word "evangelize."[3] The verse could just as readily read:

"Go into all the world and evangelize the whole creation."

In mission circles it is common to speak about three degrees or methods of evangelizing. Evangelism can happen silently through a believer's winsome presence; it can happen by proclamation; or it can happen by persuasive appeal to someone to become a follower of Christ.

By his mention of the word "proclaim" as imperative, Jesus is discounting the use of silent "presence" of a believer as being enough to evangelize. The world will never be won through the silent presence of believers, no matter how admirable their conduct may be. Along with a winsome presence must be a vocalization of the message. There must be a conveying of the good news about Jesus, challenging sinners to repent of their sins and place their trust in him for a pardoned life now and eternal life hereafter. Believers are tasked to appropriately proclaim the gospel, with the expectation that some people will listen, be convicted and then be persuaded to believe.

In 1974 the Billy Graham Evangelistic Association sponsored the Lausanne Congress on World Evangelization. That congress formulated the following explanation of the nature of evangelism that has become a guidepost in missions since then:

> To evangelize is to spread the good news that Jesus Christ died for our sins and was raised from the dead according to the Scriptures, and that as the reigning Lord he now offers the forgiveness of sins and the liberating gifts of the Spirit to all who repent and believe. Our Christian presence in the world is indispensable to evangelism, and so is that kind of dialogue whose purpose is to listen sensitively in order to understand. But evangelism itself is the proclamation of the historical, biblical Christ as Saviour and Lord, with a view to persuading people to come to him personally and so be reconciled to God. In issuing the gospel invitation we have no liberty to conceal the cost of discipleship. Jesus still calls all who would follow him to deny themselves, take up their cross, and identify themselves with his new community. The results of evangelism include obedience to Christ, incorporation into his Church and responsible service in the world. (I Cor. 15:3,4; Acts 2:32-39; John 20:21; I Cor. 1:23; II Cor. 4:5; 5:11,20; Luke 14:25-33; Mark 8:34; Acts 2:40,47; Mark 10:43-45)[4]

Unquestionably the overall goal and highest stated priority of Jesus is World Evangelization – the kind mentioned in the Lausanne Covenant. Whatever plans, programs, or activities missions engage, all are to be measured against this priority. As missions engage in proclamation, discipleship, church planting and a host of necessary support ministries, all should promote the progress of world evangelization. There is no nobler goal to which an ambassador of Christ is called; there is no clearer vision that he or she must have. Although a variety of other synonyms and even catchy mottos can be found stating what the core mission of the Church is, from this verse it can be said that "world evangelization" states it best. Evangelism should always be considered the lifeblood of the missionary movement. The mission of the church has evangelism as its highest priority. Every other activity falls beneath this ultimate goal.

Evangelize!

All five Great Commission passages allude to what is meant by evangelization without directly defining it. When all is considered and taken into account, these along with other passages would support a description of world evangelization as follows:

> The process of communicating the gospel of Jesus Christ in culturally sensitive ways, so that all peoples everywhere might have the opportunity to repent of their sins and place their faith in the redemptive work of Jesus for the salvation of their souls.

When this is the genuine response, followers of Christ should then commit themselves to becoming lifelong disciples of him. The goal of evangelism is to see sinners who are hopelessly lost in their sin accept Christ as their Savior and Lord.

When it comes to world evangelization, let's be realistic as to what is involved. Missionary statesman Dick Hillis stated a generation ago, "It is not our responsibility to bring the world to Christ; but it is our responsibility to take Christ to the world."

> This is the decision we do not make, because it has already been made. Whether we spend our lives for the purpose of reaching all men with the gospel is not optional. Christ has commanded every Christian to do just this. Now there are many different ways of accomplishing this one purpose – but regardless of the particular work God has for each of us to do, the one aim of us all in doing our particular job for the Lord must be the evangelization of the whole world.
>
> – G. Allen Fleece

The highest priority of every believer should be taking Christ to the world, no matter what specific "niche" of this mission God has entrusted to him or her. The means employed are many, the methods applied diverse, the missionaries sent vary in gifting, training, and skills, and the money expended is enormous. But the overarching goal – world evangelization – is one and the same.

Henry Crocker has portrayed this goal well in his inspirational poem, "Evangelize!"

Evangelize!

Give us a watchword for the hour,
A thrilling word, a word of power,
A battle-cry, a flaming breath,
That calls to conquest or to death;
A word to rouse the church from rest,
To heed her Master's high behest,
The call is give: ye hosts arise,
Our watchword is Evangelize!

The glad evangel now proclaim,
Through all the earth in Jesus' name;
This word is ringing through the skies,
Evangelize, Evangelize!

To dying men, a fallen race,
Make known the gift of gospel grace;
The world that now in darkness lies,
Evangelize! Evangelize![5]

Is Evangelizing ever a sin?

It is clear that world evangelization is of utmost importance. But, does this give believers permission to conduct evangelism any old way they want? No, it does not. Some overzealous activities may be sinful, and those caught up in them likely aren't even aware of it.

Yes, some are shocked to question whether any effort to evangelize could ever be sinful. How could it be possible that intentional outreach, the centerpiece of world evangelization, could at times be wrong? After all, is not the primary responsibility of believers to evangelize all peoples, in all places, at all times, at all costs? With that as a given, how could it be suggested that evangelism could ever be ethically wrong or downright sinful? To think so would be paramount to pulling the plug on the Great Commission itself!

I remember arriving years ago on the Indonesian island of Papua (then called Irian Jaya) as a rookie missionary. I soon learned that churches of another "Christian" group down the coast had better church attendance than we did in my mission's area. How shocked and dismayed I was to learn that their success was built on their missionaries' practice of enticing villagers to church by free handouts at the end of services. As the villagers exited the church door, they were each given a handful of tobacco. No wonder they had better attendance! A giveaway, no matter how small, went a long way in a society of subsistence living.

As disturbing as this revelation was, I was equally appalled to learn that 150 years earlier the first Protestant pioneer missionaries to the island, who pre-dated the other group, had done the very same thing. They actually had set the precedent of giving tobacco handouts in exchange for church attendance. The Papuan "tobacco Christians," were no different from the better known "rice Christians" of China, where, instead of tobacco, rice was the preferred inducement gift given by some missionaries.

Just how ethical is the use of material incentives to gain new converts? Is it deemed proper to give material assistance before, during or after people have come into the Christian fold? Just how skewed are our numbers when trying to determine who the true believers really are as compared to those who join church activities based on material rewards? Do the ends justify the means?

...when God spoke to us in Scripture he used human language, and when he spoke to us in Christ he assumed human flesh. In order to reveal himself, he both emptied and humbled himself. That is the model of evangelism which the Bible supplies. There is self-emptying and self-humbling in all authentic evangelism; without it we contradict the gospel and misrepresent the Christ we proclaim.

- R. W. John Stott

Hindus in India don't think so. In isolated instances over recent months they have risen up violently against neighboring Christians, accusing them of using bribery and coercion to make converts. In most instances, they have grievously misunderstood the Christian application of compassion ministries. In others, they have a legitimate gripe.

Or take a related ethical issue. To promote their political agenda, at times governments can misconstrue legitimate missionary evangelism for their propaganda purposes. Not long ago Venezuelan President Hugo Chavez expelled American missionaries from the country for "using proselytism of remote tribes as a cover for espionage." Although these charges never had credibility, why did Chavez use a misconstrued ethical issue as an excuse to justify his actions?

One thing is clear. Outsiders everywhere are looking in on missions, waiting to pounce on missionaries with the slightest excuse if it can be inferred they use ethically questionable evangelism. No matter how thin a case they may muster, they are watching and waiting to accuse.

This being the case, it is incumbent on missionaries to make concerted efforts to keep evangelism above reproach. When evangelistic zeal is not matched with moral integrity, we do deep harm to the credibility of the gospel. We even make it abhorrent to the unconvinced. Thus, to put it bluntly, we make evangelism a sin.

Unethical evangelism can manifest itself in numerous forms – listed here are only a few.

1. Evangelism is a sin when evangelistic methods are offensive to the human spirit. Those to whom we proclaim the gospel need to be seen first and foremost as human beings created in the image of God. While it is true they are also sinners in need of conversion, they still have worth and dignity and should be approached as having such. If we are aggressive, manipulative, abusive, underhanded, lacking in integrity, demeaning, offensive, confrontational, insensitive, distorting, and provocative in our witness, then we are offensive.[6] In 2 Cor. 1:14-16 Paul says that we are the aroma of Christ to those who believe, but a "smell of death" to those perishing. This stench should always be due to the gospel itself, not because of the unethical means by which it is presented.

2. Evangelism is a sin when it is exploitative. This occurs when enticements and inducements are coupled with the gospel message. While there may be times when compassion, health and help ministries accompany proclamation, these should never be construed as manipulative and coercive to those we are seeking to reach. Leaders of other religions especially see right through these enticements and take offense. Subsequently they may put pressure on local authorities to shut that kind of "evangelism" down. If they fail in doing that, they will grumble about it in their circles, stirring up trouble. In the long run more harm than good is done when these tactics are employed.

3. Evangelism is a sin when the gospel is peddled for self-serving purposes. In 2 Cor. 1:17 Paul speaks of those who would peddle the gospel "for profit" rather than "with sincerity, like men sent from God." In the world of missions, that "profit" manifests itself not only in possible monetary gain, but also includes the unscrupulous use of inflated statistics, an undeserved reputation for oneself or an organization, boasting in accomplishments, or

positioning for praise and acclaim. Wrong motives are at the root of each of these selfish outcomes and all are obviously self-promoting rather than God-pleasing. When there is greater concern for the status and reputation of an organization than for the salvation of souls being served, the outcome is self-serving sin.

4.   Evangelism is a sin when it mirrors unscrupulous methods of other religions. Islam, Hinduism and even some threads of Buddhism are also missionary religions. Adherents are schooled in methods of outreach just as we are. The Christian evangelist must guard against copying unethical methods many times employed by these religions that humanly speaking, give them an unfair advantage. Islam has its *dawa* or mission to convert the world. In places like Indonesia *dawa* efforts include the promise of the building of mosques in each village that converts to Islam. Furthermore, by strategy Muslim men intentionally marry Christian girls with the goal of turning Christian areas Muslim. In some places in India, militant Hindu priests zealously go around to villages forcibly 'reconverting' Christians back to Hinduism. Many times this activity is accompanied by bold threats against those who resist. By contrast the Christian evangelist should not be threatening or conniving. Rather, one should emulate the apostle Paul who was, "gentle…like a mother caring for her little children" (1 Thes. 2:7), and "as a father deals with his own children, encouraging, comforting and urging you to live lives worthy of God." (1 Thes. 2:11-12).

5.   Evangelism is a sin when it is insensitive to peoples' feelings. Don't get me wrong – we need to be bold in our witness just as Paul claimed to be "very bold" in his (2 Cor. 3:12). Yet at the same time in every cultural situation we must exercise sensitivity to our audience (1 Cor. 9:19-23). If our boldness lacks cultural sensitivity and ignorance of worldviews, it will be offensive. Therefore, our witness must be seasoned with grace. And grace means taking a humble, non-confrontational approach to evangelism. Evangelism is graceful if it is open, welcoming, serving, loving, caring, affirming, honest, trusting, vulnerable, attractive, sensitive, and respectful.[7] It is grace-filled when it takes the time to study and observe local customs and traditions. This is evangelism that is Christ-like. This is evangelism that appeals to the unregenerate heart.

Can evangelism, the imperative of Mark 16:15 ever be a sin? Yes, it can. When methods and motives are wrong, it is sinful. When it is insensitive to local customs and norms, it is sinful. When it is manipulative and exploitive it is sin-filled.

In our zeal to evangelize the lost, our methods should never discredit the glorious message we proclaim. While it may be true that the messenger himself may be discredited, the message should never be – and it won't be if ethical standards are followed. The apostle Paul told the Corinthian believers that our message will be offensive to some. As emulators of Christ, we must make every effort to ensure its delivery is not.

Determined Thomas

At the beginning of this chapter, we saw Jesus taking time to convince Thomas that he was indeed the risen Lord. Jesus had good reason to focus on Thomas. He foresaw the potential this man had to become one of the most outstanding cross-cultural evangelists among the eleven.

Thomas, for his part, took every word of Jesus to heart from this encounter. He then acted upon them. From doubting Thomas he was transformed into "determined Thomas." He became determined to fulfill the mission of Jesus to the extreme Jesus had just spoken about.

Not long after Jesus' ascension, Thomas began to make his way eastward. He traveled further and wider than any of the other apostles. According to church tradition, Thomas crossed countries, kingdoms, continents, rivers and penetrated into diverse religious communities to herald the gospel. He did not stop until he reached one of the most extreme parts of the earth then known to man. He kept on going for thousands of miles until he made his way to what is today southern India, a remarkable journey for that era! There he died a martyr's death, and that is probably the only thing that kept him from going even further. But he left a trail of believers in his wake! Today, there is an established ancient church in southern India that traces its heritage back to the apostle Thomas.

What drove Thomas to go so far? What motivated him to reach as many people as possible? What transformed him from being doubtful into a determined person? One single sentence from the mouth of the resurrected Jesus motivated him:

"Go into all the world and proclaim the gospel to the whole creation."

What Jesus wants you to know as you go...

Jesus lost one disciple (Judas) during the Passion Week, and he didn't want to lose another. He took extra effort to convince Thomas of his resurrection, because he knew the potential this man had to convince others in far away places of his saving grace. As it turned out, he was right – Thomas became a bold cross-cultural witness, taking the gospel to the ends of the earth. Perhaps you also are such a person.

The disciples needed to know how important the message of redemption was to all of mankind. They needed to understand that all peoples everywhere were to hear this message. The magnitude of the task was not lost on them. They were to take the gospel into all the world and proclaim the gospel to the whole creation. Both the global extensiveness of the task and the person-by-person "personable-ness" of the task was made clear to them.

World evangelization, the process of communicating the gospel of Jesus Christ in culturally sensitive ways, so that all peoples everywhere might have the opportunity to repent of their sins and place their faith in the redemptive work of Jesus for the salvation of their souls, is the goal of this evangelistic mandate.

In our zeal to evangelize we can be unnecessarily offensive and even counter productive. We need to guard against engaging in unethical evangelism.

The Building Blocks of the Great Commission

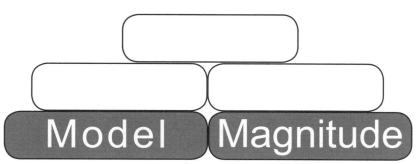

Chapter 4

The Methodology for Mission

T he brief accounts of Jesus' post-resurrection appearances to his disciples cannot include everything Jesus said when he was with them. He likely spent hours speaking to them, mentioning additional things not included in the Gospel records. One thing he must have told the disciples during the encounter mentioned in Mark was that they were to meet him again on a specific mountain in Galilee, just as was pre-announced by the angels at the tomb (Mt. 28:7).

It would be at least a three day walk from Jerusalem. So, having two encounters with their resurrected Lord behind them, they left Jerusalem and made their way north to Galilee. They were all too happy to get there. This was their home territory. Every disciple originated from Galilee (Acts 1:10), except Judas. Galilee is the place they would feel most safe, away from the hostile environment that still loomed back in Jerusalem because of their connection with the condemned Jesus. The mountain air and lapping Sea of Galilee would therapeutically soothe whatever lingering trauma they were experiencing.

The eleven likely took some time to meet with their families before proceeding to the mountain Jesus had designated for their meeting. Why did Jesus choose this isolated, out-of-the-way place? We often see in the Gospels that whenever Jesus wanted to impart important instructions to his disciples, he did it in a retreat setting. Many times his place of preference was on a mountain. There they were able to avoid interruptions from the crowds and distractions of family. In these more intimate settings Jesus had their undivided attention.

There was good reason why Jesus especially wanted this isolated retreat setting for the next installment of his commission. This was to be his most detailed missional instruction of the five. World evangelization hinged upon them fully comprehending the details he was about to pass along to them. At this time he would relate to them the specific methodology he wanted them to employ as they carried the gospel to the ends of the earth. He wanted to make sure they got it right. At this meeting Jesus was very intentional and most exacting as to what their task would entail.

Why was the Apostle Matthew the one who recorded this, the most extensive and detailed commission of Jesus? When we recall Matthew's previous profession the answer is not difficult to discover. Matthew had been a tax collector before becoming a follower of Jesus (Mt. 9:9-13, 10:3). As such he was skilled in keeping records. His livelihood depended upon accurate bookkeeping. Because of the exactness of details found in this passage, it is not hard to imagine that possibly Matthew, with parchment and stylus in hand, took notes on what Jesus told the disciples at this gathering. In all likelihood he kept those notes until a later date when he would incorporate them into his fuller Gospel.

The Commission that is Great

Open any English version of the Bible and you will discover the heading "Great Commission" inserted somewhere in Matthew 28. Some Bibles have it before verse one. Others put it ahead of verses sixteen or eighteen. All have the phrase somewhere, even though it is clear the heading was never part of the original text. Centuries after Matthew penned his Gospel, Bible translators inserted it into the body of text to guide readers into understanding the far-reaching implications of this passage.

Commenting on this phrase, Patrick Johnson claims that a theology of mission by the proponents of the Great Commission has often been "too simplistic and lacking in comprehensiveness." He then adds that the phrase "Great Commission" has been overexploited by those committed to its implementation, and ignored by the rest of the Church.[1] Whatever the case may be, the heading has been part of this chapter for nearly 500 years.

In this instance the adjective "great" is an appropriate modifier of "commission." Of all the commissions found in Scripture, none compare to the greatness of this one. None are as far-reaching in authority, task, scope, methodology, and promise as this. What's more, obedience to it through the centuries has caused devout followers of Christ to expend an extraordinary amount of time, resources, prayer, sacrifice, and effort. Truly, it shows itself to be "great" in many respects.

Great in authority

It is a common mistake for some to think that this commission begins with verse 19. That seems to be where most people begin when they quote it. But by beginning there, it omits one of the most important assurances Jesus could pass along to his disciples and those who would follow after them. He begins the commission by saying,

"All authority in heaven and on earth has been given to me" (verse 18)

The commission is great in authority. Authority is different from power. One can wield a lot of power yet not have proper authority to do so.

I have three grown sons who, when they were younger, could not wait for the day that they could out-wrestle dad. Over time, as their bodies developed into teenagers, they finally could take down and even pin dad. Each was elated when he could exercise power over me – the one who had exercised power over him all his life! However, as a face-saving measure, I would remind each of them, as I slowly pulled myself off the floor, that although he could now exert more power than I, it was I who still had ultimate authority. I was the one who still made the rules of the house. I could still tell them what to do and not to do and when to do things. Though I was no longer stronger, I still had ultimate control through my authority.

During his final meeting with them, recorded in Acts 1, Jesus would remind the disciples of the power available to them. For now, he needs them to understand that his absolute all-inclusive authority was the underpinning for their engagement in world evangelization. The right for them to go on mission anywhere, enter any country, encounter any culture or witness in any community to persuade any person to believe on him was a God-given right based on his authority. Therefore that right was indisputable. It was this authority that gave Peter the boldness, when questioned about his witness, to say to the Jewish religious leaders, "we must obey God rather than men" (Acts 5:29). What audacity! But Peter's audacity was based on divine authority he had received from Jesus himself.

When Jesus mentioned this authority, it probably prompted the disciples to recall the words of the prophet Daniel when in a vision he saw a preview of God's authority:

He was given authority, glory and sovereign power; all peoples, nations and men of every language worshipped him. His dominion is an everlasting dominion, that will not pass away, and his kingdom is one that will never be destroyed. (Daniel 7:14)

That the mandate has its origin in God whose sovereign rule is over all creation is significant to the Great Commission. It is significant because it precludes that no man anywhere, no matter what his position of authority, can ever rightfully claim that the mission of the church is invalid or unjustified. No church anywhere can claim exemption from it, and no government of any country at any time can justify suppressing it. The mission given to the Church is irrevocable and unstoppable. The propagation of the Good News of Jesus Christ is God's sanctioned plan for this era in human history, and he stands behind it.

The realization that God's authority transcends all others and underpins the Great Commission, has important practical implications:

For the missionary

The missionary has the ongoing confidence that what he is doing is authorized by God, and not based on his own will, inclination, initiative, or plans.

For sending churches

The sending church can know with certainty that her mission to the world is totally worthwhile and worthy of her efforts and resources (personnel, prayer, projects, money).

For the receiving Church

Receiving churches, wherever they be found (including here in North America), need to recognize that foreign assistance from fellow believers is to be welcomed and utilized as it advances toward maturity, autonomy and capability to also reach out. Outside assistance is to be accepted not on the basis of availability, nor because it is charitable, but because the provision has been authorized by God himself.

For governments

No matter what the country or who the leader, those placed in governmental authority need to recognize that the Christian mission is not a form of foreign imperialism, nor is it a meddling in their internal affairs. Nor are God's ambassadors who are in their country a guise for a foreign "spiritual ploy," menacingly disrupting local communities. Rather, missions is something that has been mandated from a higher authority than they themselves possess. Missionaries enter their countries on no less a basis than on the authority of Almighty God who has sent them there.

In this regard Herbert Kane says it like no other:

> The Great Commission then, is based on the supremacy and sovereignty of Jesus Christ, the Son of God, who in the Incarnation became the Son of Man, that through His death and resurrection He might become the Savior and Sovereign of the world. He is not only the Head of the church and the Lord of the harvest; He is also the Lord of history, the King of the nations, and the Arbiter of human destiny. Sooner or later all men must come to terms with Him. He and He alone has the right to demand universal allegiance."[2]

Great in task

Jesus next tells his disciples what the specific task of his mission is to be:

> "Go therefore and make disciples of all nations, baptizing them in the name of the Father, and of the Son and of the Holy Spirit, teaching them to observe all that I have commanded you." (Matthew 28:19-20)

If there is a focal point to the Great Commission, then this is it. In the previous chapter in was noted that evangelism is the highest priority of Jesus' mission. Now, Jesus tells what specific outcome that evangelism is to have – making disciples. What that means and how it is to be done is clarified by Jesus.

An examination of the grammar shows that this sentence consists of four verbs. It consists of an imperative tied to three accompanying participles with modal force. The principle verb of the sentence is not the first one "go" but rather the second one "make disciples." The centerpiece of Jesus' command is the making of disciples.[3] The intent of the sentence becomes clear when diagramed as follows:

Therefore

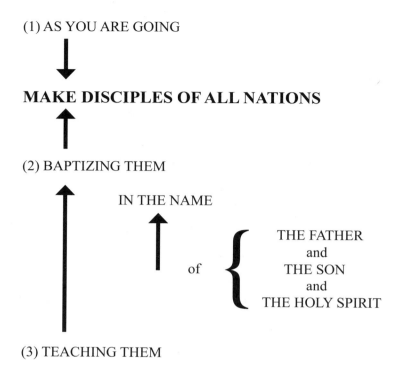

(1) AS YOU ARE GOING

MAKE DISCIPLES OF ALL NATIONS

(2) BAPTIZING THEM

IN THE NAME

of $\left\{\begin{array}{c} \text{THE FATHER} \\ \text{and} \\ \text{THE SON} \\ \text{and} \\ \text{THE HOLY SPIRIT} \end{array}\right.$

(3) TEACHING THEM

TO OBEY EVERYTHING I HAVE COMMANDED YOU.[4]

"Make disciples"

Robert Coleman has stated, "The ultimate goal of Jesus for his disciples was that his life be reproduced through them into the lives of others."[5] The making of disciples is more than just the making of converts. Evangelism is not complete when a person gives a simple assent to the gospel message. The raising of a hand, the walking of an aisle, an uttering of a sinner's prayer is not the culmination of the Church's task. It is only the beginning. Granted, the good news is shared, and it is believed, but the mission doesn't stop there. Evangelism initiates the process of a person becoming a consistent follower of the Savior in whom they now believe. But this is not the making of disciples or "discipleship" as some put it.

George Barna offers a succinct definition of a disciple. He defines one as "becoming a complete and competent follower of Jesus Christ."[6] Discipleship then is the process where mature believers build personal relationships with new believers for the purpose of producing growing and competent followers of Jesus

Christ. The process develops over a period of time and demands the building of relationship.

Producing authentic, lifelong followers of Jesus is the goal of making disciples. These individuals evidence their genuineness in the faith by their progress in spiritual maturity that transforms their beliefs and behavior. Thus I suggest an appropriate definition of a disciple to be:

> A consistent lifelong follower of Christ whose life is progressively being transformed into the image of Christ's. He joyfully walks with Christ, is constantly being informed by Scripture, prayer, the Holy Spirit and other believers, with the chief end of glorifying God.

I like the way George Peters describes it: "discipleship is a path rather than an achievement. While there is growth and grading among the disciples, there are no graduated disciples. Discipleship is a perpetual school which may lead from one degree to another but does not graduate its scholars."[7]

The disciples understood firsthand what this discipleship process entailed. Over the past three years Jesus had lived with them, walked with them, and told stories to them. They followed after him and fellowshipped with him as everyday experiences became lessons on loving God, loving others, and denying self. Thus they would have intuitively understood that all he had modeled to them, they were to likewise do for others.

Jesus goes on to tell the disciples that making other disciples is a three-step process: first by going to those who had had no exposure to the gospel; second, by calling them into a relationship with Jesus that culminates in baptism; and third by teaching them to observe his commands.[8]

> The command has been to 'go,' but we have stayed -- in body, gifts, prayer and influence. He has asked us to be witnesses unto the uttermost parts of the earth ... but 99% of Christians have kept puttering around in the homeland.
> – Robert Savage

"Go"

The first step in making disciples is to go to where there are people who are not Christ followers. Placed first in the sentence it shows it is the first step, and actually since it is linked with "make disciples" carries a mild imperative force.[9] This is the third time the disciples heard they were to go somewhere. It shows the duty of believers to take the gospel from where it is known and believed to where it is not known or believed.

The verb can readily be translated "as you go," indicating concomitant circumstance. This is a reminder that in every experience of life, all believers should be sensitive to the presence of others around them who are in need of the gospel.[10]

"Baptizing them"

Jesus doesn't mean to use baptism as a magical rite that automatically brings people into relationship with him without a change of heart. Sadly, it has deteriorated into that very thing in some church traditions. Rather baptism is the culmination of the repent-believe-baptize experience of salvation.

This public symbol of initiation is very meaningful. It is a picture of beginning a new life in Christ and of allegiance to him and to his church. The ordinance is a powerful outward expression of a new identity and a changed life within. Indeed because of these implications, there are new believers in some hostile cultures who delay its application for fear of repercussion. Antagonistic nonbelievers understand its significance!

That believers are to be baptized in the name of the Father, Son, and Holy Spirit indicates the believer's new relationship with the triune God. The names of the three persons of the Trinity are invoked in baptism to show the significance of all three in the salvation experience. God the Father is the author of grace, Jesus the provider of grace, and the Holy Spirit the applicator of grace. The three work together in harmony to bring lost souls to the place of redemption. This Christian rite rightfully recognizes all three persons of the Godhead, and teaches the new believer that this is the God who now is to be worshipped. Baptism then pictures all that is implied when a person repents of sin, believes in Christ and is placed into the fellowship of believers.

"Teaching them"

The making of a disciple does not stop with the initiation experience. There is an educational process that follows to keep the new follower learning and growing in his new faith. Some today would equate this with "spiritual formation." Whatever the label, the important thing is that there is an ongoing growth experience. A new believer's worldview must be changed; his lifestyle adjusted to increasingly conform to the image of Christ; and his ethical conduct increasingly marked by integrity. When transformation is apparent in these areas, that believer in turn is in a position to teach others and thus duplicate the process.

Teaching has a final goal – obedience. New believers are taught with the goal that they become obedient followers of all Christ commanded. Among other things that Jesus taught, they are to live out the great commandment (Mat. 22:37-40) and show great compassion (Mat. 9:36). It takes growth experiences in community with other believers for this to be most effective.

This is why believers are congregated into churches (and why some have labeled this passage the "church planting" commission). This is why missionaries have established Bible schools and seminaries the world over. This is why seminars, webinars, church-based training and a host of other teaching ministries are so important. Growth happens best in the presence of other believers. It is the local church that best facilitates the fellowship of believers. Iron sharpens iron and one man sharpens another (Proverbs 27:17). Therefore, by implication the establishment of local congregations is an outcome of the methodology for mission.[11]

Superficial or genuine outcomes?

Thus, all three activities – going, baptizing, teaching – are necessary components to transformational discipleship. When done correctly, lives are genuinely changed. This is the ultimate objective of making disciples – the transformation of lives. However, the lack of genuine changed lives is the greatest omission of the Great Commission the world over. All too often "proselytes" are made instead of "disciples." When this happens churches get filled with bodies who exhibit little evidence of changed beliefs and behaviors. This results in spiritually apathetic "believers" who quickly deteriorate into nominal Christians. And nominal Christians, although they wear the tag "Christian" are not Christ-followers at all. They are superficial followers of "the way" in need of a conversion experience.

This sad state has become the bane of the Church the world over. It causes skepticism when it comes to the validity of certain church planter's reports. Although it is common to read reports about myriads of conversions and prolific church planting movements, what is the value of those reports if they do not evidence the bearing of fruit of transformed lives? Superficial conversions and inflated statistics only promote non-authentic outcomes.

It is incumbent on God's messengers to engage in a process of making disciples that has the transformation of lives as the final goal. Only then are people genuinely disciples of Christ. Only then is the intended outcome of the Great Commission achieved "among all nations."

Great in scope

What specifically did Jesus mean when he said "all nations?" The immediate response would indicate that Jesus seems to be speaking of the geo-political "nations" wherein mankind dwells. At present, according to the United Nations' count, there are 238 "nations" on our globe. Is this what Jesus meant by reaching the nations? If so, it could be argued that a good share of people have been reached in every nation, and therefore the accomplishment of the Great Commission is nearly, if not already, complete.

But, the phrase *panta ta ethne* is a more technical phrase (*panta* = all, *ta* = the, *ethne* = nations) with a more precise meaning. At the Lausanne Conference on World Evangelization of 1974, Ralph Winter brought to the attention of the attendees that the task of making disciples of the nations is much more involved and much greater in scope than simply reaching geo-political nations. He argued from this passage and others that Jesus intended the phrase to be understood in the sense of ethnic groups or people groups. It is better to see the human race divided into their ethno-linguistic groupings, rather than the artificial divides into which humans have politically divided themselves.

Subsequently, the meaning of a people group was refined in 1982 by the Lausanne Strategy Working Group as

> a significantly large grouping of individuals who perceive themselves to have a common affinity for one another because of their shared language, religion, ethnicity, residence, occupation, class or caste, situation, etc. or combinations of these...the largest group within which the Gospel can spread as a church planting movement without encountering barriers of understanding or acceptance.[12]

Jesus intends for people to be converted and made disciples from every people group, rather than from entire nations collectively. A survey of the biblical use of the term from Genesis to Revelation bears this out.

One of the first encounters of this phrase is in Genesis 12:3. Abraham was to be a blessing to "the nations" (*panta ta ethne*). The Greek translation of that phrase in the Septuagint is exactly as it is found here in Matthew 28. The blessing from Abraham would reach into every ethno-linguistic group on earth. Of course this could only happen through a distant descendent of Abraham, namely Jesus, who would be the blessing to the entire world.

The phrase is used in various other places in the New Testament, including the Luke commission passage (Luke 24:47). In Revelation, the phrase takes on a clearer definition as two visions of the future make-up of peoples around the throne of God are portrayed by John.

Revelation 5:9 and 7:9 assume the central missionary task of reaching people groups has taken place by the end times. The use and order of the specific terms in the two passages are compared as follows:

Rev. 5:9	Rev. 7:9
tribe	nation
language	tribe
people	people
nation	language

Although the word order is different, these terms describing people groups are identical. These verses not only refer to the universality in the spreading of the gospel, but also to the depth in societies where the gospel will reach.

One last heavenly vision is found in Revelation 15:3-4. This "song of Moses" and "song of the Lamb" is the great doxology sung by the myriads who come out of the tribulation period victorious. The words of this song are significant in relation to the extent of world evangelization. In it victorious peoples praise God by singing:

> Great and marvelous are your deeds, Lord God Almighty.
> Just and true are your ways, King of the ages.
> Who will not fear you, O Lord,
> and bring glory to your name?
> For you alone are holy,
> All nations (*panta ta ethne*) will come and worship before you,
> for your righteous acts have been revealed.

Just how many ethno-linguistic groups are there today? Several counts have been given, but it is probably most accurate to say that there are 16,302. Of these 9,653 are considered "reached," as counted by the Joshua Project.[13] John Gilbert has defined "unreached" as: "An ethno-linguistic people within which there is no viable indigenous church planting movement with sufficient strength, resources, and commitment to sustain and ensure the continuous multiplication of churches."[14]

The scope of Jesus' mission is vast. He is telling his church that its evangelistic task should not be considered complete until there will be a representative from every ethno-linguistic group praising God in heaven.

Great in promise

Jesus closes his instruction with the most tender of assurances meant to encourage the hearts of those who would engage in the Great Commission. He leaves the disciples with the promise that he will always be with them as they spread the good news far and wide. This can be called "the comforting clause" of the Great Commission, as those words were intended to do just that – bring comfort to any who engage in world evangelization. Jesus promises:

> "And behold, I am with you always, to the end of the age."

Jesus knew that in a few short weeks he would leave the disciples permanently. But because of his abiding spiritual presence with them after his ascension, he promises to go with each of the eleven as they in turn go on their various mission outreaches.

Although the impact of this promise was not realized at the moment, what a comfort it must have been to the disciples as they later fanned out across the globe. That same promise gives comfort and assurance to Christ's ambassadors today as they forsake all and leave their homelands for the sake of the gospel.

Although "end of the age" has been translated "end of the world" in earlier translations, this temporal rendering is more accurate than a geographical one. It is the same word from which we get our word "eons." Though this may be a technical point, it is reassuring to know that even more than at any place, Jesus is with his messengers at all times in every age. His ongoing presence is promised right through to the end of time. There is no place they will go where he will not be present, no time when he will be absent. The omnipresent and eternal nature of Jesus guarantees this promise always to be true.

Probably no other prayer says it better than the one attributed to the famous medieval Celtic missionary, Patrick. Read closely the words of confidence this poem invokes.

"The Breastplate of St. Patrick"

I arise today through a mighty strength, the invocation of the
Trinity, through belief in the Three-ness, through confession
of the Oneness of the Creator of creation.

I arise today through the strength of Christ with His Baptism,
through the strength of His Crucifixion with His Burial
through the strength of His Resurrection with His Ascension,
through the strength of His descent for the Judgment of Doom…

I arise today, through God's strength to pilot me:
God's might to uphold me, God's wisdom to guide me,
God's eye to look before me, God's ear to hear me,
God's word to speak for me, God's hand to guard me,
God's way to lie before me, God's shield to protect me,
God's host to secure me:
against snares of devils, against temptations of vices,
against inclinations of nature, against everyone who
shall wish me ill, afar and near, alone and in a crowd.

I summon today all these powers between me (and these evils):
against every cruel and merciless power that may oppose
my body and my soul:
against incantations of false prophets,
against black laws of heathenry,
against false laws of heretics, against craft of idolatry,
against spells of women [any witch] and smiths and wizards,
against every knowledge that endangers man's body and soul.
Christ to protect me today:
against poison, against burning, against drowning,
against wounding, so that there may come abundance of reward.

Christ with me, Christ before me, Christ behind me, Christ in me,
Christ beneath me, Christ above me, Christ on my right,
Christ on my left, Christ in breadth, Christ in length,
Christ in height, Christ in the heart of every man who thinks of me,
Christ in the mouth of every man who speaks of me,
Christ in every eye that sees me, Christ in every ear that hears me.

I arise today through a mighty strength, the invocation of the
Trinity, through belief in the Three-ness, through confession of the
Oneness of the Creator of creation.
Salvation is of the Lord. Salvation is of the Lord.
Salvation is of Christ. May Thy Salvation, O Lord, be ever with us.[15]

Charles Spurgeon summed up the teaching of this commission found in Matthew with the following: "This is the perpetual commission of the Church of Christ; and the great seal of the Kingdom attached to it, giving the power to execute it, and guaranteeing its success, is the King's assurance of his continued presence with his faithful followers."[16]

What Jesus wants you to know as you go...

Jesus did not want his followers to be timid in spreading the good news of his redemption to the world. Rather he wanted them to give a bold witness, assuring them that they had the authority to go anywhere at anytime based on the fact that the mandate had come from God himself.

As they went, their evangelistic efforts were to culminate in the making of disciples; i.e., consistent life-long followers of Jesus whose lives are increasingly being transformed into the image of Christ. New followers were to be baptized and then taught to observe Christ's commands and demands on their lives in the context of Christian community – the church.

The task should never be considered completed until there are thriving believers found in every ethno-linguistic group on earth. This means going beyond the geo-political borders by which mankind has divided itself, right into the heart of every ethnic group found within those borders.

As they go, Christ's messengers do not need to feel they are doing this task alone. Jesus' comforting presence will be with them at all times, right up to the end of this age. There is no place they will go where he will not be present, no time when he will be absent. The omnipresent and eternal nature of Jesus guarantees this promise to be true.

The Building Blocks of the Great Commission

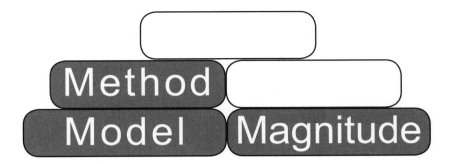

Chapter 5

The Message of Mission

Beginning with the evening of Resurrection Day, Jesus had met off-and-on with his disciples at various locations over a forty-day period. He had two primary objectives for those meetings: 1) to convince them by way of many irrefutable proofs that he was indeed alive and had experienced a bodily resurrection (Acts 1:3) and 2) to prepare them for their next assignment. They were close to graduating from being followers (disciples) to becoming global ambassadors (apostles). As the very first "sent ones" of his, they would become the pioneer bearers of the Good News.

As a master teacher, Jesus knew that if the disciples were to fully comprehend his instruction about the mission, it would take reinforcement through repetition. He also knew that the critical nature of the task he was asking of them was best grasped by incrementally imparting the information. The overarching goal – world evangelization – was not to be lost on them.

At this meeting recorded by Luke, Jesus' goal is to clarify the message they were to herald to the nations. The value of his redemptive work and it becoming known to all mankind, depended upon them being convinced about it themselves.

It was mentioned previously that evangelization can be relegated to three components: presence, proclamation and persuasion. The life example of a believer exhibiting a moral Christ-centered life (presence), coupled with a verbal witness (proclamation), culminating in urging others to appropriate for themselves Christ's work of grace (persuasion), encompasses evangelism.

The information Jesus has passed along to his disciples up to this point comprises the core of evangelism. Notice the "three p's of evangelism" embedded in the Great Commission passages Jesus has given so far:

"As you are going"

Presence ⟶	Proclamation ⟶	Persuasion =	World
"so send I you"	"preach the gospel"	"make disciples"	**Evangel-**
(John 20:21)	(Mark 16:15)	(Mat. 28:18-20)	**ization**

Jesus knew that the activity of evangelization, although important, in and of itself was not enough. It needed substance. It needed to be connected to a relevant message that met a dire need. He also knew that the importance of that message needed to be clearly understood if the disciples were to devote the rest of their lives proclaiming it. Therefore his intent at this fourth encounter is to ground them in the essence of the message they were to proclaim.

Need for the message

When you stop and think about it, ambassadors of the gospel in all ages have a lot of audacity. They have the audacity to leave their homeland to live cross-culturally in other countries and cultures. They have the audacity to proclaim a strange message to the peoples of that culture. They also have audacity to challenge followers of other belief systems to abandon those long-held beliefs and embrace a new set of convictions. Many times this new message is as foreign to the hearer as the person who brings it to them.

> Men are in this plight not because they are unevangelized, but because they are men. Sin is the destroyer of the soul and the destruction of the knowledge of God which is life. And it is not the failure to have heard the gospel which makes men sinners. The gospel would save them if they heard it and accepted it, but it is not the ignorance or rejection of the gospel which destroys them, it is the knowledge of sin.
> – Robert E. Speer

The gospel is rarely automatically believed when heard for the first time. One mitigating reason is that the worldview of a culture is informed by the belief system that has become the warp and woof of that society for generations. Another factor is that the meaning of a message across cultures many times gets distorted in its transmission, causing the message, at least at first, to become incomprehensible.[1]

But these factors aside, the deeper reason for non-acceptance of the gospel is a societal concept of mankind's root problem or predicament. The belief of man's root problem varies from ethnic group to ethnic group. It is inescapably linked to the belief system that undergirds a society. A cursory survey of the world's major religions bears this out.

Animism
Over 200 million of the earth's inhabitants are animists.[2] Animistic peoples consider unseen spirits that permeate the world around them as the culprits for their spiritual and physical plight. Their worst nightmare is to have a spirit or band of spirits antagonize them or bring them harm. Their energies are focused on appeasing the spirit world through ritualistic practices. Since there is no high god to assist them, they must help themselves by manipulating the spirit world as best they can. As such, this is a religion of practical humanism.

Hinduism
Hindus view their spiritual predicament a little differently. Although spirits need to be contended with, for them ignorance is the greater cause of deep-seated human problems. If they only were better enlightened, they would know how to be delivered from their problems. Therefore better knowledge, combined with the ritualistic appeasement of multiple gods and spirits, delivers one from his or her's nagging spiritual predicament.

Buddhism
Buddhists take this matter a step further. For them suffering is the greatest human predicament, and the primary cause of suffering is human desire. Unchecked desires cause the greatest of problems and the deepest of sufferings. Therefore, following Buddha's four noble truths that extend into his eight-fold path will bring control to human desire.

Islam
On the other hand, Muslims believe selfishness to be at the core of man's predicament. Allah's wrath falls on those who, out of selfishness, refuse to submit to him. This is manifested by wrongdoing on man's part. Therefore, one needs to work feverishly to rid oneself of the weight of those wrong deeds. By so doing, Allah will be appeased. The way to do that is by submitting to him (the word Muslim means "one who is submitted") through constant engagement in five fundamentals or "pillars" of belief and practice. On the merits of consistent

engagement in these, a person can save himself. This makes Islam the most autosoteric among all religions.

Judaism
Finally, the modern day Jew has his own idea of his predicament. Jews are found grouped into a variety of branches that hold to various levels of orthodoxy. A common thread that runs through this religion is the belief that broken relationships are the root cause of the Jew's deepest problems.[3] It is therefore incumbent upon the Jew to mend broken relationships and maintain good ones at all costs. Relationships of most concern are those between family members, within communities, between adherents of other religions, and with God.

All of these beliefs have something in common with Christianity. They all focus on an aspect of life that is of deepest concern to believers in Christ as well – man's spiritual predicament. However, that is where the similarity stops. As widespread as the representation of predicaments found among them is, none go far enough in pinpointing man's true root problem as revealed in Scripture.

To use a medical metaphor, in its own way each religion focuses on a symptom of man's deepest problem, but not on the disease itself. Each concerns itself with external circumstances which it attempts to control through rituals and religious practices. Sadly, all fall short of what Scripture pinpoints as man's real root problem – that of sin. Thus, the need for believers to proclaim a lucid message is imperative. Jesus knew this and used this opportunity in Luke 24 to teach the disciples the essence of the message that is to be proclaimed.

The Message

Jesus knew that his good news message would be as applicable to the pluralistic environment of the 21st century as it was to that of the first and every century in between. He also knew that in its simplest form it needn't be theologically complicated. He understood what words of help and hope would resonate with human needs, no matter what culture they lived in or worldview they possessed.

Therefore at this fourth post-resurrection encounter, Jesus told the disciples to proclaim a message that was succinct yet meaningful to any person living anywhere in any culture. Its relevancy to everyone and anyone was not to be lost on the disciples. All that a person needs to know is encompassed in one sentence:

> Then he opened their minds to understand the Scriptures, and said to them,

"Thus it is written, that the Christ should suffer and on the third day rise from the dead, and that repentance and forgiveness of sins should be proclaimed in his name to all nations, beginning from Jerusalem."

In brief, Jesus makes four vital statements that comprise the essence of the gospel message:

1. Who Jesus is: the promised Messiah (Christ)
2. What Jesus did: suffered death and raised to life
3. How one is to respond: repentance
4. What benefit is gained: forgiveness of sin

Put another way, the gospel includes three essential truths:

1. The reality of sin as man's greatest predicament.
2. The redemptive work of Jesus as the only cure for that predicament.
3. The response of repentance that is necessary for a sinner to be forgiven of sins.

These three truths encompass the essence of the gospel message. These are all a person needs to know to experience a right relationship with God. These are all that are necessary to have a salvation experience.

The message expanded

As concise as the gospel message is, Jesus took the opportunity to expound on that information. By so doing he was both laying the underpinning of that message and assuring its propagation to all peoples.

1) Message basis – Old Testament Scripture

"Thus it is written." The gospel has never been a stand-alone message that was concocted by either Jesus or his disciples. It is a message rooted in the Old Testament Jewish Scriptures. The story of redemption began in Genesis, developed throughout the Old Testament, and then found its fulfillment in Jesus – the promised Messiah. It is a message reinforced by Old Testament imagery and prophecy. Jesus' sacrificial death for sin was the apex of God's redemptive plan that had begun centuries before.

2) Message core – Christ suffered and raised

Part 1: Christ suffered
There was only one way that the totality of God's holiness and justice could be met and satisfied. Only through the uniqueness of Christ's personhood

and atoning work could that be done. The one and only perfect Son of God dying for sin once for all could only do that. In his death Jesus paid the price for sin, freeing God up to offer forgiveness to sinful man (2 Cor. 5:21). Paul states it as, "God was in Christ reconciling the world to himself" (2 Cor. 5:19). In Christ's suffering all the requirements of God's holiness, justice, love and mercy were met (Romans 3:25-26).

Part 2: Christ raised
The resurrection of Christ from the dead proved he was divine and the sole provider of salvation. This is the centerpiece of the Christian message: the bodily resurrection of the historical Christ. The validity of the entire gospel story rests on the reality of Jesus' bodily resurrection.

For the apostles who saw and fellowshipped with him after the resurrection, this became the bedrock of the gospel. All the Gospel writers conclude their accounts of the life of Christ with accounts of Jesus risen from the dead. This became the dominant theme of all preaching and teaching in the infant church. In Acts its reality was woven into all gospel presentations (Acts 1:2,25; 2:22-36; 3:15; 4:10,33; 5:30; 7:56; 9:4; 10:40; 13:30-37; 17:3, 31-32; 22:7; 26:14).[4]

3) Message requirement – repentance
The repentance (*metanoian*) that is to be proclaimed carries a specific meaning. It is used to denote the need to "have another mind" by changing one's opinion about something. As Thrasher notes, "true repentance has intellectual, emotional and volitional elements. Intellectually, it involves a change of mind about God, sin, Christ and oneself. The resultant change of mind views God as good and holy; sin as evil and injurious before God and people; Christ as perfect, necessary, and sufficient for salvation; and oneself as guilty and in need of salvation. Such repentance is an essential element of missionary proclamation."[5] Man's repentance is necessary for salvation, but is not meritorious in and of itself. It is his response to Christ's death that fully satisfies God's righteousness requirement (Romans 3:25). Repentance is the non-negotiable response to the gospel message.

4) Message provision – forgiveness
The Christian message is a glorious message of pardon. God has granted full pardon from man's nemesis – namely sin. When a person repents, he is freed from the penalty of sin, the power of sin and in future glory from the presence of sin. The extent of forgiveness is total and eternal! It takes care of his past, the present, and the future.

The word carries the idea of "dismissal" or "release." It is intended to show a deliverance or liberty that comes through a legal pardon. God suspends, or "sends away" for all eternity the just penalty of sin on behalf of the repentant sinner.[6] The punishment due mankind was paid for by Jesus (Romans 5:6-10, Eph. 2:13).

Thus, forgiveness of sins is at the very heart of the Christian message. There is no other message like it anywhere in the world. No other religion promises full pardon either in this life or the next. No other religion completely cures man's spiritual predicament. No other religion can say with confidence, "There is therefore no condemnation to those who are in Christ Jesus" (Romans 8:1).

5) Message necessity – sin as man's spiritual predicament

The sin nature found within every human being is the root spiritual predicament of all mankind. There are no exceptions. Scriptures tell us that man is sinful by nature, by birth and by choice.[7] Sin is more than moral failure on man's part. It is "missing the mark" of God's righteousness altogether. It entails rebellion against the very person of God.

Sin is so deeply ingrained in the soul of human beings that there is no one who has the ability to rectify the problem in and of themselves. Its roots penetrate so deeply into the human heart that its ugly head keeps appearing and reappearing no matter how hard man tries to beat it back. Because of his predicament, man forever manifests his sinfulness through ignorance, desire, wrongdoing, broken relationships and fear of spirits.

What's more, man fails miserably in his attempt to conquer these and other selfish manifestations. That is why Jesus came to the rescue. That is why he wants his message of rescue known. That is why our message is so important. That is why Jesus could so confidently say to the disciples on the evening of his betrayal that he alone was "The Way and the Truth, and the Life" (John 14:6).

This leads us back to the world religions and their varied ideas of man's predicament. They also have their varied responses to what can be done.

Animist:
The animist is basically clueless and would ask the question, "what way, what truth, what life?"

Hindu:
The Hindu would say, "discover a way, discover a truth, discover a way of life" among the pantheon of gods that permeate his religion.

Buddhist:
The Buddhist would suggest that one "follow a way, follow a truth, and follow a way of life" as prescribed by the Buddha.

Muslim:
The Muslim, on the other hand would say that a person is to "submit to a way, submit to a truth, and submit to a way of life" as dictated by the prophet Mohammad through the Koran and Sharia law.

The Jew:
Finally, Jewish people would say one is to "build a way, build a truth, and build a way of life" that promotes wholesomeness across the broad spectrum of human relationships.

Notice that each of these religions prescribes a way of self-deliverance, based on meritorious works. But, none of them gets to the root problem of the human heart. Only Jesus provides both the answer and the provision to man's spiritual predicament. That is why he could boldly say that he alone is the "way" out of sin, told the "truth" about sin, and provides the only "life" free from the penalty of sin. Jesus alone fully and eternally takes care of man's sin problem.

6) Message extension – to all nations
Here Jesus uses the exact phrase that he did at his previous encounter with the disciples. "To all nations," discussed in the preceding chapter, has "beginning in Jerusalem" attached to it to show both the extent of where the gospel is to be carried, as well as from where it was to start.

The disciples were no doubt tempted to return to their home area of Galilee and begin their mission there. That would have been the natural thing to do. Jesus knew that if they did return home, they might never have gone out on the mission. Once back with family and friends and their fishing gear, it would have been very tempting for them not to engage the mission at all.

The mission had to begin in Jerusalem. There were clear advantages as to why it needed to begin there. One advantage was to reach as many Jews as possible from all over the empire. Many Jews from all over would be converging on Jerusalem in a few days to celebrate the feast of Pentecost. Many would hear and believe the sermon of Peter (Acts 2). Those that responded would then jump-start the spread of the gospel to all nations when they returned as new Christ-followers to their countries of residence.

Another reason for them staying in Jerusalem was so they would have maximum impact on the center of Judaism. This is where the truth of the gospel had a chance of being encountered by the most important and astute of the religious leaders. Jesus foresaw that many of these influential leaders would themselves one day believe (Acts 6:7).

Probably the most important reason to stay in Jerusalem was because it would be the place where the Holy Spirit would corporately fall upon them. The empowerment needed for the task would come through this "Other Comforter," the other person of the Triune God. Once his baptism was experienced, they would be free to proclaim the gospel as widely and as far as they were led.

Empowerment for the task

Thus, once briefed on the essence of the message, Jesus told the disciples not to go anywhere until they were first properly equipped, "But stay in the city until you are clothed with power from on high." Jesus could not overemphasize the importance of this empowerment. He knew that it was such a crucial means to world evangelization that he mentions the enabling of the Holy Spirit three times in the five commissions.

He hinted about it at the first meeting on Resurrection evening, when, speaking symbolically and prophetically, he breathed on them and told them, "Receive the Holy Spirit" (John 20:22). He mentions the empowerment again here, using the symbolism of being "clothed" by the Holy Spirit (Luke 24:49). He will mention it one last time at his farewell address with them in a few short hours (Acts 1:8).

Today, as then, the work of mission can only be effectively carried out through the supernatural enablement of the Holy Spirit. Only he can empower and energize believers for the task that in every respect is far too daunting and dangerous for them to accomplish on their own. The disciples on hearing these words, probably called to mind the words of the prophet Zechariah to another person (Zerubbabel) who too had been given a commission: "Not by might, nor by power, but by my Spirit, says the Lord of hosts" (Zech. 4:6).

What Jesus wants you to know as you go...

The message of redemption is vitally important. Every religion has its view of what man's spiritual predicament is, but all fall short of pinpointing what it really is – man's sinfulness. Man's sinful offenses against God, by nature, by birth, and by choice have resulted in alienation from God. That broken relationship can only be mended by belief in the redemptive work of Christ on man's behalf.

This message of redemption is based on the Old Testament revelation of God. At its core is Christ's death and resurrection. All that man is left to do is to appropriate by faith Christ's work on his behalf for himself. If he does he will experience forgiveness of sins, solving his nagging spiritual predicament.

This message is for all peoples. For good reasons, it started by being propagated from Jerusalem after the disciples were empowered by the Holy Spirit. From there it began its journey to the nations, being disbursed far and wide, first by the Apostles and then by those who have come after them.

The Building Blocks of the Great Commission

Chapter 6

The Means of Mission

The time had finally arrived for Jesus to leave his disciples permanently. One last meeting was all he needed to relay his final instruction. Over the past forty days he has been progressively leading them into an understanding of what he was asking of them when it came to his global mission. Now, one last piece of vital information would complete all he needed them to know before they got started.

His farewell address recorded in Acts 1 is really a continuation of what he had told them earlier in the day in an upper room in Jerusalem (Luke 24). With that session completed, Jesus now had them join him on a 2-mile trek outside the city to the slopes of the Mount of Olives (v. 12). The town of Bethany lay at the foot of that mount (Luke 24:50). After clarifying some teaching about the timing of the Kingdom, his final words were brief:

> "But you will receive power when the Holy Spirit has come upon you, and you will be my witnesses in Jerusalem and in all Judea and Samaria, and to the end of the earth" (Acts 1:8).

That was it! With that he vanished into the air right before their eyes, never to be seen face-to-face again. No wonder they lingered, gazing intently upward until interrupted by "two men in white robes" (Acts 1:10).

If those parting words had been stand-alone instructions unattached to the previous four commission statements, the disciples would have been left standing dumbfounded. Instead, since they had been recipients of a succession of instructions, they clearly grasped what Jesus meant.

In this final instruction, Jesus relayed three means of how the mission was to be carried out. These are the means of empowerment, the means of a strategic plan, and the means of human instrumentality.

The Means of Empowerment

The need for spiritual empowerment

The Holy Spirit is the divine Empowerer of missions. His coming imparted the divine enabling to every aspect of the mission enterprise. As Robert Glover has said, "Christian missions are no human undertaking, but a supernatural and divine enterprise for which God has provided supernatural power and leadership."[1]

It is the tendency of the human heart to rely on its own self-confidence and abilities for success in ministry. We easily mislead ourselves into thinking that human achievement can bring about spiritual results. But Jesus knew otherwise. He knew the spiritual battle that would ensue with the propagation of the gospel story. He also knew that the apostles were in no way equal to the task without being empowered from on high. They would not only wrestle against flesh and blood, "but against the rulers, against the authorities, against the cosmic powers over this present darkness, against the spiritual forces of evil in the heavenly places" (Eph.6:12). That is why he told the disciples:

> "But you will receive power when the Holy Spirit has come upon you..."

An important principle in missions is clear: spiritual work takes spiritual power to achieve spiritual ends. In light of this principle, it is imperative that we, like the disciples, be assured of where the source of power for mission originates.

What about management and technology?

In this highly pragmatic and secular-humanistic age, it is easy to rely on managerial missiology to achieve missional goals.[2] The mission endeavor often deteriorates into a solely human endeavor with superficial results. It becomes purely human achievement and humanistic when based on self-sufficiency. All too often organizational efficiency replaces spiritual efficacy, resulting in a flurry of activity lacking genuine results. Back in the 1970's John Stott, cognizant of this propensity of the human heart, looked ahead to our present day and insightfully wrote:

> Some people seem to look forward with relish to the time when the evangelistic work of the church will be computerized, the whole job will be done by machines instead of people, and the evangelization of the world will be the ultimate triumph of human technology.[3]

Stott was a prophet of the times! How often have we heard it said that now that we have mastered the internet, cable TV, computer programs, text messaging, and whatever else that may come along, we finally have the ability to evangelize the world. Granted, these technologies do assist in the task, but they can never replace the place and power of the Holy Spirit in world evangelization.

> ...enablement implies that we have no ability whatsoever. We're entirely powerless. We can do nothing. But when by faith we renounce self-sufficiency and embrace reliance on the power of the Holy Spirit, we receive divine empowerment, enablement, and strength for personal transformation and ministry.
> – Jerry Bridges

Power

Jesus had already assured the apostles about the authority they had been granted for mission (Matthew 28:18). That overarching authority gave them the right to go anywhere and at anytime to engage in world evangelization. Now, he informs them of the power (*dynamis*) available to them through the presence of the Holy Spirit.

The disciples knew they would be at a disadvantage without Jesus physically present by their side. It was an assurance to them, therefore, to know that another divine member of the Trinity would be with them and do for them what they could not do in and of themselves. By his power they would have the courage to preach the gospel effectively and to work miracles that would confirm the gospel message.

Holy Spirit power

In the midst of the modern climate of self-confidence built on technological achievement and corporate managerial acumen applied to missions, it is refreshing to hearken back to the disciple's humble reliance on the power of the Holy Spirit. They believed that man, being dead in the trespasses of sins, blinded to spiritual truth and enslaved to unrighteousness, could never save himself out of the clutches of Satan. They knew that only the Holy Spirit could liberate such a person from the bondage of sin, bringing him from death into life.[4] It could only be by the empowerment of the Holy Spirit that the task of taking redemption to a sin-sick world could be achieved. Like us, they needed that empowerment.

> Christians will faithfully fulfill their missionary calling only if they do God's mission in God's way. Such mission has its origin in God the Father. Jesus knows that if His disciples are ever going to faithfully carry out the demands of mission, they cannot depend merely on themselves.... We need the Holy Spirit. Our own personal resources are valuable, but they are not sufficient.
> – Neville Callam

Throughout the book of Acts the Holy Spirit's empowerment was repeatedly manifested in relation to the mission of the church. He was so intricately involved in empowering the apostles throughout every aspect of their missional journey that his presence cannot be missed. As they and others engaged the world, we see the Holy Spirit empowering for:

1. Clear public proclamation of the gospel (Peter in Acts 2:14-41).
2. Bold defense before authorities (Peter in Acts 4:8-22).
3. Directing them to prepared hearts (Philip meeting the Ethiopian in Acts 8:26-40, Peter meeting Cornelius in Acts 10:19-21).
4. The selection of new missionaries (Church of Antioch in Acts 13:1-4).
5. Confronting spiritual forces (Paul confronting Elymas in Acts 13:9-12).
6. Settling theological issues resulting from the advance of the gospel into virgin territory (Jerusalem Council in Acts 15:23-29).
7. Directing the steps of missionaries: Guidance as to where to go (Paul compelled by the Holy Spirit to go to Jerusalem in Acts 20:22), and where NOT to go (Paul in Asia in Acts 16:6).
8. Guiding in the selection of leaders for mission churches (Acts 20:28).
9. Insight concerning future experiences a missionary would encounter (Paul told in advance about being taken captive in Jerusalem in Acts 21:4-11).

The empowerment of the Holy Spirit is such a dominant theme in the book of Acts, that some have proposed that the better title for the book would be "Acts of the Holy Spirit."[5] In the apostolic church, as it should be today, the power of the Holy Spirit in mission was at the center of every endeavor.

George Peters says it well when reflecting on the importance of the Holy Spirit in missions:

> It is clearly implied and understood from the context and the general tenor of the Bible that such a task can be carried through only in the power of the Holy Spirit. He is the great Superintendent, the Energizer and Sustainer of His church. The church's task, in the final end, is a supernatural task which demands supernatural resources. Because these are available in the Holy Spirit we must lean hard upon him.[6]

The Means of a Strategic Plan

The book of Acts is a historical record of the geographic, linguistic and ethnic expansion of the gospel. Acts 1:8 doubles as a table of contents for the book. The gospel was first preached among the Jews of Jerusalem and Judea (Acts 1-8), and then to the mixed-Jews of Samaria (Acts 8-12), and finally to the Gentiles everywhere else (Acts 13-28). However, there are other aspects of mission that Jesus teaches in this command as well.

No one center

The nature of the global mission of the church demands that it should never establish one geographic center. Jesus, wanting to make sure the disciples did not establish Jerusalem as its center, explicitly told them to go out from that city. The Old Testament version of centripetal mission, where Israel welcomed all nations streaming to it, was to be replaced by the centrifugal mission of going out to the nations. Christianity was not to be an ethnically Jewish-centric religion, a linguistically Hebrew-centric religion or a geographically Jerusalem-centric religion. The straightjacket of one culture was not to be imposed upon it.

As such, Christianity was not designed to be a Jewish *"axis mundi"*(center from which everything revolves) religion. Freedom from this concept would permit it to flourish anywhere in the world and in any culture in which mankind lives. The idea of a holy, centralized center of religion was not to be part of this new faith.

The genius of Christianity would be that God could genuinely be worshipped wherever believers were found and in ways culturally appropriate to them. The concept of Christianity having a multitude of centers throughout the world would become the *modus operandi* that would permit this new belief to thrive.[7] The reality that Jerusalem initially did become a center of Christianity was to have a short life span by design. This may be an extenuating reason God allowed its destruction in AD 70. There was to be no permanent center![8]

Three places simultaneously

Another thing Jesus made clear was that the witness of the apostles was to take place in three arenas simultaneously. They were to have a witness in their capital city, Jerusalem, and in the immediate environs of Judea; subsequently radiate to the half foreigners in Samaria, and then go far beyond Palestine to the end of the earth.

Some assume the spreading of the gospel was to be a three-step process: first to Jerusalem and Judea, then on to Samaria, and finally stretching to the end of the earth. But to the contrary, the language of the text points to a simultaneous witness in all three areas at the same time. The verse literally reads:

"...in Jerusalem *and* in all Judea *and* Samaria *and* to the end of the earth."

The "ands" don't mean "then to" or "next" as though Jesus was advocating a strategy of successive steps. All regions are to have our attention and efforts simultaneously. This same strategy is important in today's globalized age of exponential international migration where peoples from every people, tribe, tongue and nation are criss-crossing the world right up to our doorstep. Our witness needs to be right **here** where we are, it needs to be **near**by, and it needs to be **over there** at the same time.

A missiological parsing of Acts 1:8:

This verse also gives a glimpse into the dynamics involved when the gospel travels from place to place and culture to culture. For the disciples starting out from the city of Jerusalem, the paradigm is portrayed in the following chart. For those of us involved in missions today, notice the dynamics that all cross-cultural workers need to pay close attention to in regard to ethnicity, geography, language and culture as the gospel goes forth:

Dynamic	Jerusalem and all Judea	and Samaria	and to the end of the earth
Ethnicity	Their own people	Mixture of Jew and Gentile	Other peoples altogether
Geography	Their own capital city and regional identity	Neighboring region	Far away places
Language	Their native language (difference in accent only)	Different dialect	Completely foreign language
Culture	Their own culture	Slightly different culture	Totally different cultures

Three types of evangelism

Ralph Winter in his historic address at the 1974 Lausanne International Congress on World Evangelization has done more than any other in this generation to help believers understand the missiological paradigm Jesus gave in Acts 1:8. In that address Winter pinpointed the three types of evangelism needed to reach the world today. He labeled those three types E-1, E-2 and E-3 evangelism.[9]

E-1 evangelism takes place when a person stays within his own people group, geographic area, own language and culture to win people to Christ. This typically happens when a Caucasian American witnesses to another Caucasian American living just down the street. With most everything in common between them, the task of communicating together is relatively easy and without barriers.

In E-2 evangelism the task is not as simple and requires different techniques. The bearer of the gospel crosses into a different, but usually nearby geographical area to reach people who speak a different yet understandable dialect, who are living within a slightly different culture. The cultural and linguistic barriers crossed are relatively simple to navigate. A believing Navajo going to the Apache would be an example.

E-3 evangelism requires a more complicated communication skill set because of higher barriers that need crossing. In this instance, a person goes to an altogether different people, who are usually in a distant place, who speak a completely different language and operate in a completely foreign culture. The missionary must engage in language acquisition, cultural adaptation and worldview comprehension before he is able to present the gospel with clarity and effectiveness. The task is considerably more difficult than E-1 or E-2 evangelism, and demands special training. A Canadian going to the Lisu people of southern China would be an example.

Although there are differences in the complexity of task, E-1, E-2 and E-3 are to be seen as equal in value. With this explanation, another look at the Acts 1:8 parsing reveals the following:

Dynamic	Jerusalem and all Judea	and Samaria	and to the end of the earth
Ethnicity	Their own people	Mixture of Jew and Gentile	Other peoples altogether
Geography	Their own capital city and regional identity	Neighboring region	Far away places
Language	Their native language (difference in accent only)	Different dialect	Completely foreign language
Culture	Their own culture	Slightly different culture	Totally different cultures
Type of Evangelism	**E-1 Evangelism**	**E-2 Evangelism**	**E-3 Evangelism**

E-1 evangelism is powerful, but E-2 and E-3 evangelism are essential to completing the task of world evangelization. Fully one-third of the world's 6.9 billion people cannot be reached unless the church engages in E-3 evangelism. Another third that are "close by" cannot be reached without E-2 evangelism. Winter has aptly said that, "We are forced to believe that until every tribe and tongue has a strong, powerfully evangelizing church in it, and thus E-1 witness within it, E-2 and E-3 efforts coming from outside are still essential and highly urgent."[10]

The Means of Human Instrumentality

My witnesses

One last comment needs to be made about the disciples' (and our) personal involvement. Jesus put at the heart of this command the phrase:

"...and **you** will be **my witnesses**..."

Human instrumentality is the God-ordained means of reaching out to humans. No other way, avenue, or being was enlisted by God to do this task. It must be humans evangelizing other humans for this mission to be most successful.

British missionary William Carey, "the father of modern missions," had to convince a denomination of reluctant Baptists to get involved in world evangelization. To convince them of its importance, he wrote a pamphlet that used the word "means" in its title. After discussing the importance of the "means" of prayer, he wrote: "We must not be contented however with praying, without *exerting ourselves in the use of means* for the obtaining of those things we pray for. Were the children of light but as wise in their generation as the children of this world they would stretch every nerve to gain so glorious a prize, nor ever imagine that it was to be obtained in any other way."[11]

The disciples had been eyewitnesses of Jesus' life and ministry from the very start. These men had spent three full years with him which allowed them to observe him under every conceivable circumstance. They witnessed every miracle he performed and heard every address he gave. They saw his concern for the lost, his compassion for the unfortunate, and his care of the needy. They listened to his beautifully crafted parables, and saw him dumbfound his critics by his wisdom. And in the end they watched as he suffered and died, but also met him several times after he victoriously rose from the dead. For them, it was indisputable that Jesus was the Son of God.[12]

Thus the disciples needed no persuasion that Jesus' words and works were of God. They had witnessed every aspect of his life and ministry. They were there as eyewitnesses when all those marvelous things transpired. Indeed, he was that "which we have heard, which we have seen with our eyes, which we looked upon and have touched with our hands" (1 John 1:1). As eyewitnesses they could testify to the veracity of all Jesus' mighty acts.

When Jesus told them that they would now "be my witnesses," he was telling them that they were to proclaim what they had personally experienced with him. Their story was linked to their identification with him. Their first-hand experiences would lend credence to their message.

Over the centuries the meaning of the word "witness" (*martures*) has evolved in Christian circles. It has moved from its original generic meaning of "somebody who saw or heard something happen and gives evidence about it" to the more specific meaning of "a public statement of strong personal Christian beliefs." Because so many believers have died doing that very thing, the word eventually took on the meaning of "martyr." A martyr is a believer who has lost his life prematurely in a situation of witness, as a result of human hostility.[13] Every one of the disciples except one would die a martyr's death. (See map in Chapter 9 pinpointing where they served and died.)

This is the kind of witness Jesus would have us doing today. Christ's mission to the nations can only go forward as believers proclaim what they themselves have personally experienced with Christ. It is those believers who boldly give public affirmation about their salvation experience and believe in it so strongly that they are even prepared to die a martyr's death that pushes missions forward. This is what Jesus' disciples ended up spending the rest of their lives doing. This is what believers in every age should be willing to do as well.

What Jesus wants you to know as you go…

The daunting task of world evangelization that lay before the disciples would take more muscle than they could ever muster in and of themselves. As well trained as they were after spending three years with Jesus, they lacked the one important ingredient that would enable them to go on mission with confidence. They needed the supernatural empowerment from a higher source, the Holy Spirit. He alone would enable them to carry on the task. Jesus was now ready to send the Holy Spirit to them as he left them permanently.

Just before his final departure, he told them about the strategic means in which the gospel was to go forth from Jerusalem. First they were to proclaim it within their own general environs. Then they were to take it across ethnic barriers to nearby peoples. Finally they were to cross over into foreign cultures and peoples who were vastly different then themselves. But as they went farther and farther, they were not to forget the previously evangelized areas. Simultaneously, these were to have their attention as well.

The gospel message is applicable to all peoples everywhere at all times. It is a supra-cultural message that finds meaningful acceptance wherever it is proclaimed. Therefore, the disciples' task was not complete until they had carried it to the uttermost parts of the earth. And if they failed to complete that task in their lifetime, then those who followed after them were to pick up where they left off.

It takes individuals with firsthand experience with Christ to proclaim with passion his salvation to the nations. This is why only genuine believers qualify for the task. This is why we find that the most mission-minded churches today that are committed to world evangelization are comprised of those who have experienced for themselves new life in Christ. They are "witnesses" in the true sense of the word.

The Building Blocks of the Great Commission

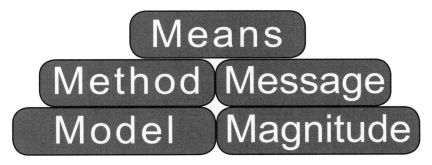

Conclusion to Part 1

With these final words found in Acts 1:8, Jesus brought his instruction to a close. He has finished telling his disciples everything they needed to know to get the mission started. They have completed five training sessions which were incremental, systematic, exacting, and comprehensive. No topic was left uncovered, no part left unclear. They had it all. They knew with certainty what was expected of them and what they were commissioned to do.

After Jesus' ascension, although they were saddened by his going, they were neither timid nor directionless. Instead, they were just the opposite. Once baptized by the promised Holy Spirit a few days later, they became emboldened and purposeful. They gladly and boldly inaugurated a mission to the world that has been ongoing ever since.

Slowly at first, and then with ever increasing momentum, they began to fan out across the Mediterranean world and beyond. All of them engaged in mission for the rest of their lives, carrying the gospel north, east, south and west from Jerusalem, their starting point. Once they had served and died, others picked up the task after them carrying the gospel even farther. And then others did the same after them and that ongoing process has continued right down to the present. Now this generation is tasked to do the same.

When you think about it, we are the fruit of the labors begun by the disciples. The gospel has been passed along through twenty centuries right down to us. We must ask ourselves, "What new additional fruit will our generation bring in?" This depends on how much we value and follow the Great Commission as given by Jesus. As was stated in the Preface: *It is not that believers don't know about it; it's that many don't know how to go about it.*

PART 2

Prologue to Part 2

The disciples stood on the mount gazing intently into the sky in awe and wonderment. A minute earlier, Jesus had been standing and calmly talking to them. A moment later, he began to slowly rise off the ground into the air and then, after a brief pause that permitted a parting look, he was out of sight. He had disappeared right before their eyes! After a prolonged stare with faces steeled upward, they turned their attention back to earth and began discussing among themselves the amazing rapture they had just witnessed.

"I think he has left us for good," James said breaking the silence.

"Yes," added John, "He's gone permanently this time, and he left in such an amazing display of power and glory. His departure appeared so triumphant! Did you notice how regal he looked as he left?"

"He finished what he came to earth to do. His work is completed," Nathanael chimed in. "It was time for him to go. Now it is up to us to spread word about his amazing life and works." The others nodded in agreement.

"Before we do anything else, I really feel the need to spend some time debriefing our experiences we had with him," cautioned Thomas. "We especially need to hash over these past several weeks where he repeatedly told us what he expects us to be doing now that he has left."

"Yes, that's a really good idea. I think we need to pull together his final instructions so we don't miss a single detail," answered Matthew – always so exacting. "If we don't, we are likely to make a mistake or leave something out, or not do anything at all."

"I'm for that," Peter agreed. "Let's head back to the city and meet at our regular place to talk things out. We should do that before we do anything else. It will really help if we tie together all those instructions he gave us."

With that, as dusk began to fall, the disciples started down the dusty road that led into Jerusalem. When they reached the city gate, they split into groups of twos and threes so as not to be conspicuous. In divided clusters they made their way through the narrow, curved streets, past shops, stands and animal stalls to the room they had been renting over the past several weeks. It did not take long before they were all assembled. Once they had washed their feet and refreshed themselves, they took their familiar places.

Then methodically, one-by-one, they began to piece together all they had heard from Jesus over the past forty days…

Chapter 7

The Great Commission Diamond

Jesus gave the Great Commission to his church through his disciples. Although these instructions are over 2000 years old, they are meant to be freshly understood and applied by every succeeding generation of believers. This must happen if his plan to redeem peoples scattered all over the globe is to be realized. Only by obedience to these words will Jesus' mission and, by implication, the church's mission, continue to go forward as he intended.

Part 1 of this book began by synchronizing Jesus' five Great Commission instructions and then examining them one-by-one to determine their unique emphases. Though an analysis of individual passages was enjoined, the overall picture can easily get lost, thereby losing sight of the grandeur of the forest because of the trees.

So as to sharpen the application of the Great Commission passages to today, we need to ask; what are the core components Jesus would have his followers to know as they go? A synthesis of the Great Commission passages reveals four essential elements that make up the core of the Great Commission. The following "Great Commission Diamond" will help illustrate these four essentials. All four are equally important, for history has proven that when any one of the four is missing or misconstrued, mission inevitably veers off course.

Why a Diamond?

Why are the four essentials of the Great Commission best illustrated by a diamond? Because of the nature of a diamond. Stop and think about it. Diamonds are the most highly prized of all gemstones. When cut and buffed they are beautifully transparent. It is the hardest mineral known to man, with many industrial applications such as in cutting tools and abrasives. When placed in jewelry, a diamond beautifully reflects light as no other gem, brilliantly sparkling as no other jewel.

In many ways these traits are identical to the Great Commission. Of all the commissions found in Scripture, this is the most highly prized. When "wielded" properly, it cuts into hardened human hearts and cultures, laying bare the inadequacies of other philosophies and religions by its transparent message. However, like industrial diamonds, it takes human instrumentality to make that happen. When held to The Light, it brilliantly reflects the light of the gospel.

With the diamond to assist, we'll examine the four essentials that make up the points of the Great Commission Diamond. These may well have been the same talking points the disciples discussed when they debriefed together after Jesus' ascension. Remember, all four are essential if we are to fully comprehend and apply what Jesus wants us to know as we go.

1. A Worthy Messenger

Messenger

God has been calling select people to be his messengers since he sent Noah to preach to his unrighteous neighbors. When God has a message to pass along, he delights in using human instrumentality for the simple fact that by so doing it incarnates his message, and thus helps it to be authentic to human recipients.

Messengers of the gospel must not only be willing to serve but, more importantly, they must be found *worthy* to serve. God cannot use instruments that are not fit for his use (2 Tim. 2:21). They must be qualified. In the context of the Great Commission instruction, three foundational qualifications of worthiness are found.

1. Prepared: "...be my witnesses" (Acts 1:8). When Jesus told the disciples that they would be his witnesses, he was telling them that they were to proclaim what they had personally experienced with him. Their story was linked to their identification with him. Their firsthand experiences would lend credence to their message. As eyewitnesses they would testify to the veracity of all Jesus had done.

   The disciples were prepared to do this because of their participation in the three-year "internship" program they had just completed. During those years Jesus had taught them what to believe and how to live out those beliefs. He modeled compassion, courage and trust in God, along with a perfect portrayal of the "fruit of the Spirit." He mentored them in his school of discipleship, leading them in the "knowing," "being," and "doing" of ministry. By the time of his ascension, they were cognitively, behaviorally, and experientially prepared to serve. Messengers must have personal experience with Jesus before going on mission for him.

   > ...when God spoke to us in Scripture he used human language, and when he spoke to us in Christ he assumed human flesh. In order to reveal himself, he both emptied and humbled himself. That is the model of evangelism which the Bible supplies. There is self-emptying and self-humbling in all authentic evangelism; without it we contradict the gospel and misrepresent the Christ we proclaim.
   > – R. W. John Stott

2. Authorized: "All authority in heaven and on earth has been given to me. Go therefore..." (Mat. 28:18-19). An individual cannot simply declare that he has a "call" to serve as a missionary and then assume others will accept that call as legitimate. His call must be validated. God uses his people – the church - to confirm such a call. It is God who sends a messenger on assignment, but He sends him or her through His mediate, visible means, which is the church. Why? Because it is the church that is in the position to recognize if a member is truly qualified for such service. That is why I find it necessary to include this element in my definition of a missionary:

   A missionary is a messenger sent by God through his church to take the gospel cross-culturally from where it is known and believed to where it is not known or believed.[1]

The phrase "sent by God through his church" implies a double authorization for a person. On the one hand, God is the indirect, immediate, and invisible authorizer of the mission. On the other, the church is the direct, mediate and visible authorizer.[2] The two work in tandem in the sending process, giving legitimacy to the person who is sent. This principle is clearly portrayed by the sending that took place at the church of Antioch in Acts 13:1-4.

3. Empowered: "But you will receive power when the Holy Spirit has come upon you..." (Acts 1:8). Perhaps this is the most noticeable missing element in the sending of messengers today. The empowerment of the Holy Spirit has in many respects been substituted by training, techniques, technology and professional skills. All of these are important and need to be part of the missionary's arsenal to do mission, but they are not a substitute for spiritual refreshment and empowerment that come from a supernatural Source.

> Christian missions is a supernatural venture. Only supernatural resources can sustain it and make it dynamic. The contact with the Divine is imperative. Prayer is not optional; it is operational and decisive.
> – George Peters

A life of purity, a penitent heart, a humble spirit and a posture of prayer through communion with the Holy Spirit, are requisite to empowerment from him. This empowerment is not a one-time experience that one might mistakenly think enables a messenger to serve throughout his entire career. Rather, it is a daily constant yielding, by faith, to his presence and control of one's life.

2. A Certain Message

Messenger

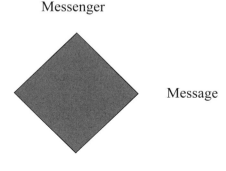

Message

Today, as in the time of the disciples, Jesus first and foremost needs his messengers themselves to be absolutely convinced about what they proclaim. It is not enough to give mental assent to a doctrinal position or set of beliefs. There must be wholehearted belief. I am reminded of what a seminary professor once said, "People don't live what they profess, but rather what they believe." The same is true when it comes to the message in missions. Messengers don't proclaim by rote what they have been taught; but they do proclaim what they believe in their heart.

In the religiously pluralistic environment in which we find ourselves, Jesus needs messengers who are fully convinced about the importance of the gospel message. The stakes are too high to send half-persuaded messengers who themselves do not fully grasp the basic tenets of that message. Uncertainty of belief makes for halfhearted and unreliable messengers. Once hardship or resistance hits, the questioning messenger typically:

- Throws in the towel and returns home prematurely, believing the demands on him, his family and calling are not worth the effort and sacrifice.

- Compromises the message so as to make it more amicable to listeners, believing there must be validity in other belief systems that are being confronted as well.

- Changes ministry priority from that of evangelism to engagement in humanitarian causes as an acceptable alternative, seen as having higher importance.

If unreached peoples are to be reached and won to Christ, then it is imperative the messenger be absolutely certain about the message he proclaims. Certainty of belief needs to be evidenced by unwavering conviction in three fundamental doctrines:

1. Bible – as authoritive (Luke 24:44-45)
    The gospel message is solidly rooted in the inspired written word of God. Every doctrine that is to be believed, every practice that is to be affirmed, every teaching that is to be taught, must squarely align with Scripture. There is no other source of truth, no other uncorrupted revelation, and no other divinely inspired written revelation from God to mankind other than the Bible itself. All other religions are out to **discover** God. Only in the Bible does God **disclose** himself to mankind.

Jesus modeled and emphasized the exclusive use of Scripture as the source of all truth in his teaching to the disciples about his unique place in redemptive history. At the time he gave his fourth commission to them (best labeled "the doctrinal" Great Commission passage), Luke records, "Then he said to them, 'These are my words that I spoke to you while I was still with you, that everything written about me in the Law of Moses and the Prophets and the Psalms must be fulfilled.' Then he opened their minds to understand the Scriptures..." (Luke 24:44-45).

Jesus used the Scriptures as the sole basis of the salvation message and plan. And so should we. Any deviation from Scripture produces deviate doctrine. Deviate doctrine produces deviate beliefs we call sects, cults, and new religious movements. Only an absolute belief in the Scripture as the sole Divine guide and rule in all matters of faith and practice keeps the Church from doctrinal error, heresy, and proclaiming a deficient gospel.

2. God – as Trinity

Jesus made it clear in his third Great Commission instruction to the disciples that they were to "...baptize them in the name of the **Father** and of the **Son** and of the **Holy Spirit**..." By insisting on that formula he was emphasizing the oneness of God in the form of three, the Trinity. Since he was linking this formula to the initiation rite of Christianity, he was marking this concept of the Divine as the root of Christian theology.

The doctrine of the Trinity means that there is one God who eternally exists as three distinct Persons – the Father, Son, and Holy Spirit. Stated differently, God is one in essence and three in person. These definitions express three crucial truths: (1) The Father, Son, and Holy Spirit are distinct Persons, (2) each Person is fully God, (3) there is only one God.[3]

Messengers of the gospel understand this unique yet all-encompassing divinely revealed concept of Deity. Although it defies full explanation, it is nevertheless proven throughout the Bible. Biblical Christianity is unique in this view of monotheism. It sees God as a plural unity with three distinct persons. Although a complex doctrine to understand, its origins come from the very words of Scripture, beginning with Genesis 1:1 where God is mentioned in plural.

In the grand story line of Scripture, the Old Testament focus is on God the Father yet the other two are implicit. The Gospels focus on God the Son yet the other two are still implicit. In Acts and in the Epistles where the focus is on the Holy Spirit, again the other two are implicit. God is three yet One.

Belief in God as Trinity is the cornerstone of the Christian faith. Without it we would have a creator God who is distant and impersonal, a Jesus who was merely an outstanding historical figure – a mere human being, and a Spirit who would be thought of as only an arbitrary natural force. Without belief in the Trinity we have a deficient view of God, which in turn makes for a deficient presentation of the gospel.

Yet many Christians today live their faith as if there were only one manifestation of Deity. Christian Schwarz has insightfully observed the three tendencies that come from three segments of the Christian church. Liberals tend to emphasize God as Father (Creation), Evangelicals tend to emphasize God as Son (Calvary) and Pentecostals tend to emphasize God as Holy Spirit (Pentecost). Schwarz states, "There are people for whom only God's revelation in creation seems to constitute what is important in Christianity; for others it is exclusively Calvary; for others again, exclusively Pentecost.[4]

A litmus test to determine if one recognizes all three persons of the Trinity equally is by one's prayer life. Do you pray to all three? Do you mention all three either in your salutation, or throughout the course of your prayer, or at least at the closing? Trinitarian prayers make for Trinitarian believers.

When it comes to confronting other religions, belief in God as Trinity is a standout issue. As Samuel Huntington has stated, the encounter of Christianity with the world religions demands a missiological apologetic that is based upon trinitarianism.[5] Practically this is manifested by the following contrasts:

- Trinitarianism is belief in a God who is transcendent, in contrast to the local menacing spirits of animism and polytheism, and also in contrast to the New Age idea of equating humans and creation with the Divine.

- Trinitarianism encompasses a belief in a personal God, in contrast to the impersonal gods of Hindu and Buddhist worldviews.

- Trinitarianism is belief in a sovereign God who lovingly cares for his people in contrast to an impersonal Allah of Islam who leaves everything to arbitrary fate and has not intervened in human history.

- Trinitarianism is belief in a God who became flesh in human form, in contrast to the strict isolationist monotheism of Judaism that does not allow for such a possibility.

Trinitarian theology understands God as a God on mission to redeem sinful man. The Father loves the world (Jn. 3:16) and sends his Son as Savior (Jn. 20:21). The Son sacrifices himself for mankind (Hebrews 10), becomes the object of saving faith (Acts 10:34-43, 17:30-31) and is now the God-man mediator (1 Tim. 2:5). The Holy Spirit makes possible the application of salvation. He prepares hearts by convicting of sin, righteousness, and judgment (Jn. 16:8). He enacts spiritual rebirth (NOT reincarnation) (Jn. 3, Rom. 8). He makes possible true worship of God without human mediation (Jn. 4). He also makes possible service to God (Rom. 15:15-19).

God the Father, God the Son and God the Holy Spirit, are all equal members of the Trinity and fully Divine. Yet they are distinct in functions within their Oneness. Christians confess this belief, not because we fully understand it, but because God has revealed himself as such throughout Scripture. That is why in obedience to him we baptize new believers in all three names (Matt. 28:19). By so doing we proclaim to the world his unique plural unity and supremacy above the other gods.

3. Gospel – as essential

Jesus commanded his disciples to "Go into all the world and proclaim the gospel to the whole creation." (Mark 16:15). The word gospel simply means "good news." And Christ-followers have good news to share! It is actually "great news" because its provides great relief from man's nagging predicament of sin, and fills man's greatest longing for a right relationship with Creator God.

Many believers struggle to articulate what is the essence of the gospel. Here is a simple exercise to help pinpoint what it is. Let's say you have two minutes to share the gospel with an unbelieving loved one who lives some distance from you. She is dying on a hospital bed with a very short time to live. What would you say? Could you twitter to her, in a clear presentation of 140 characters or less, the essential components of the gospel?[6] What would be the irreducible minimums that you would convey? Try it!

The answer is not that difficult. There are only three essential points necessary to convey when sharing the gospel. Not one of them can be missing or else the message will be incomplete. First, the problem of a person's personal sin must be shown. Second, the provision for sin – Jesus dying as a substitution – must be revealed. Third, there needs to be a statement of how to appropriate it for oneself – accepting, believing or receiving Jesus' provision. That's it! Although further clarification would be helpful, nothing else needs to be added to bring a last chance message of life and hope to a person needing to gain acceptance by God.

Referring back to the Great Commission passage found in Luke 24:46-47 (where the emphasis is on the message) the three essential components of the gospel are identified:

> "...*Christ should suffer* and on the third day rise from the dead, and that *repentance* and forgiveness of *sins* should be proclaimed..."

Man's predicament (sin), God's solution (Christ should suffer) and the necessary response (repentance) are all mentioned as comprising the essence of the gospel. Collateral matters are mentioned that elaborate on the three, but the essentials are clear.

Perhaps Mark more than any of the other Gospel writers makes the most effort to mention the gospel in the life of Christ. He tells his readers right from the start that his book is about the beginning of the gospel of Jesus Christ (1:1); that Jesus came preaching the gospel (1:14); and he calls hearers to repent and believe the gospel (1:15). Running throughout the entire book Jesus is the theme of the gospel (1:14, 15; 8:35; 10:29; 13:10; 14:9). Mark ends his book by mentioning Jesus' command that the gospel be preached worldwide (16:15).

The apostle Paul summarizes the theological underpinning of the gospel in 1 Cor. 15:3-5:

> For I delivered to you as of first importance what I also received: that Christ died for our sins in accordance with the Scriptures, that he was buried, that he was raised on the third day in accordance with the Scriptures, and that he appeared to Cephas, then to the twelve.

This theological summary includes: 1) Jesus (Christ) dying for sins, as proof of Divine intervention; 2) Jesus buried as proof of his death; 3) Jesus raised from death as proof of his deity; 4) Jesus appearing to others as proof of his resurrection. The gospel message centers on the redemptive work of Christ.

In the New Testament the gospel is not an abstract concept that has little meaning for those who do not understand it or for those who cannot bring themselves to believe it. The New Testament presents the "gospel" for the purpose of the salvation of human souls. It is good news from start to finish. It is good news for everyone. It includes:

1. A proclamation of the death, burial and resurrection of Christ on behalf of sinners.
2. A clear theological statement of the person of Jesus as Messiah and Lord, and thus qualified to bring salvation.
3. A summons to repent and receive forgiveness of sins by faith alone in the person of Christ alone.[7]

That is why messengers of the gospel can echo the words of Paul who said, "For I am not ashamed of the gospel, for it is the power of God for salvation to everyone who believes, to the Jew first and also to the Greek" (Romans 1:16).

3. A Clear Strategy

Messenger

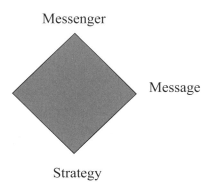

Message

Strategy

Messengers carrying a message need to know what to do with that message. It is obviously useless if a messenger, having exemplary qualifications and fully informed on the content of the message, is clueless about how to go about the assignment. Regrettably, that is the case with many Christ followers. They simply seem uninformed or misinformed about the action plan Jesus has given his ambassadors. Consequently, many good and noble works get passed off as Great Commission activity that simply don't qualify as such.

Yet Jesus made it clear what the Great Commission strategy is to be. Another look at the passages reveals three vital activities that dictate Great Commission strategy. These three activities make up the Great Commission DNA. Just as DNA is the genetic blueprint or instructions used in the development and functioning of living organisms, so these three comprise the blueprint to be followed if the Great Commission is to have success.

The DNA of the Great Commission is summed up with the acronym "EDP." The EDP strategy consists of "Evangelism," "Discipleship," and "Planting the church."

Evangelism

Evangelism is the effort of sharing the good news about Jesus to those who have yet to know him. It entails a verbal declaration of the gospel with the intent of bringing individuals to the place of making a decision to believe in Christ as the Savior from their sins.

Jesus told his disciples in Mark 16:15 that they were to "proclaim the gospel." The combination of those two words when used in tandem always means "evangelize." To help grasp the essence of evangelizing, it is good to recall what is arguably the best definition, found in the Lausanne covenant looked at previously:

> To evangelize is to spread the good news that Jesus Christ died for our sins and was raised from the dead according to the Scriptures, and that as the reigning Lord he now offers the forgiveness of sins and the liberating gifts of the Spirit to all who repent and believe…

In chapter 3 it was noted that in the early stages of giving his commission, Jesus told the disciples they were to evangelize. Evangelism is the groundbreaking part of a series of actions that make up the Great Commission strategy. It is the initial activity of the messenger. It entails presence and proclamation that leads to persuasion.

Today evangelism takes on many forms. The mode can range from personal evangelism to big-arena crusades. The techniques can range from presence evangelism to proclamation evangelism to persuasion evangelism. The technologies employed can range from a simple use of printed literature, to the use of radio, recordings, television, internet, and anything else yet to come on the technological horizon. However, no matter what the mode, technique or technology, human instrumentality will always be essential. The message will always need to be incarnated from one individual and passed on to another. The importance of human instrumentality should never be underestimated.

Discipleship

The making of disciples, or discipleship, is the accompanying strategy to evangelism in the Great Commission strategy. It encompasses all those activities which bring believers into increasing maturity in Christ. It was already noted from the study of Matthew 28:19 that "make disciples" is the principle verb and central activity of that passage. Making disciples is that activity which produces authentic, life-long followers of Jesus whose lives are being transformed as they grow in spiritual maturity.

In the early church, the Apostle Paul stood out as one of the foremost disciple-makers. The book of Acts records how he did it and what a primary focus it was in his ministry as he evangelized new areas. However, his passion for making mature disciples is probably best seen in his prayer for a group of believers he had never met. Those were the believers in Colossae who were brought to Christ by Epaphras, whom Paul had sent there.

In his prayer (Col.1:9-10) for these young believers, Paul voices a prayer that includes the essence of discipleship:

> ...we have not ceased to pray for you, asking that you may be filled with the knowledge of his will in all spiritual wisdom and understanding, so as to walk in a manner worthy of the Lord, fully pleasing to him, bearing fruit in every good work and increasing in the knowledge of God.

In this prayer of encouragement to these new believers, Paul cites each of the elements that make up transformational discipleship:

Knowing: that you may be filled with the knowledge of his will in all spiritual wisdom and understanding

Being: so as to walk in a manner worthy of the Lord, fully pleasing to him

Doing: bearing fruit in every good work and increasing in the knowledge of God

These are the elements of discipleship that are transformational. These should be the personal goals of every believer. Jesus intended these kind of outcomes in the lives of believers when he gave the "make disciples" strategy to his disciples.

Just how best to make disciples has never been universally uniform nor has a predominant strategy been agreed upon. Given the varied cultural contexts in which the gospel has been proclaimed, discipleship could never be squeezed into a one-size-fits-all straight jacket. It has rightfully been varied in methodology by Spirit-driven and creative believers throughout the church age. What works best in one culture does not mean it can be uncritically transferred to another. Each cultural setting demands its own unique discipleship application. However, it has been universally proven that the best place for making disciples is in conjunction with the local church.

Planting the church

When evangelism results in new believers needing to be nurtured as disciples, the establishment of a church is the natural outcome. Believers inherently want to band together, and when they do, a community of believers is formed that Scripture calls a church. This is why the Matthew 28:18-20 commission is many times called the "church planting commission." The process of effectively making disciples is integrally tied to the establishment of churches. Why? Because it consolidates believers into active communities.

The gathering of believers together into an assembly affords the opportunity for them to have a home base for their faith. It becomes the place of corporate worship of God, of edification, education, mutual fellowship, discipline, and the use of spiritual gifts. It becomes a base for outreach to the world, both near and far, since it is the divine institution for the propagation of the faith.

> Often people equate the word "church" with a building. However, the New Testament refers to the church not as a building, but as a body of believers (1 Cor. 12:27). The church is not somewhere we go, but something we are.
> -George Murray

Therefore, church planting is considered the focal point of Great Commission strategy. That is why Lesslie Newbigin could insightfully say, "The mission of the church is missions, the mission of missions is the church."[8] The two are interrelated and breed each other into existence.

The Great Commission strategy entails evangelism that produces converts who commit to being discipled that results in new churches. Local congregations are vital to conserving the fruit of evangelism and providing discipleship services necessary for transforming lives. This corporate bonding together of like-minded followers is a way modeled by Jesus and imitated in the Apostolic Church for global disciple-making.[9]

The local church was of vital importance to the Apostle Paul. He knew that if engagement in the Great Commission was to bear lasting fruit and if he was to be successful as a missionary, he had to channel all his fruit into the local church. Paul first demonstrated this when he was commissioned for missionary service by a local church (Acts 13:1-4).

For the rest of his missionary service, Paul attested to his strong belief in the importance of the church. He was commissioned out of a local church (Acts 13:1-4). He planted churches everywhere he went, appointed leaders to those churches for their ongoing viability, systematically revisited those churches, and wrote letters back to the churches when needed. In the process, he reported back to his sending church at the conclusion of each missionary journey.

Why did Paul make the church the focal point of his missionary endeavor? Because he knew that the strategy of the Great Commission had the planting of churches at its core. To conserve the fruit of evangelism and then be able to systematically disciple believers took a local body of believers living in corporate harmony. Thus church planting is the capstone of Great Commission strategy.

The Great Commission Strategy

Evangelism + Discipleship + Planting the Church

4. An Ultimate Goal

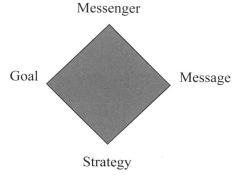

Messenger

Goal

Message

Strategy

The ultimate goal of the Great Commission can be summed up in two words: *world evangelization*. The phrase "world evangelization" succinctly summarizes what is to be the final outcome of Great Commission efforts and activities – the evangelization of the world through evangelism, discipleship and church planting.

"World Evangelization" is a popular term used in mission circles, and rightfully so. A cursory search reveals that many mission schools, training centers, mission research centers, mission buildings, mission movements (like the Lausanne Committee for World Evangelization) and conferences place the word prominently in their title. When so used, a statement is being made as to the final goal of their missional efforts and reason for existence.

The phrase "world evangelization" is not found in any of the Great Commission texts. However, we need not be alarmed nor reluctant to use it. It is fitting, based on five phrases used by Jesus in those texts. He included these five phrases to show the disciples, and the church, where the final outcome of their evangelistic efforts is to lead.

We have already encountered these phrases during the one-by-one examination of the Great Commission passages. It is sufficient here to review their meaning and then bundle them together to understand the scope of the Great Commission's final goal.

1. "all the world" (Mark 16:15): "All" being all-inclusive, Jesus told his disciples that they were to cover the entire cosmos (world) by evangelizing it with the good news.

2. "whole creation" (Mark 16:15): Along with looking at the task as being geographically global, the disciples were to see it in bite sizes and individually. Every person everywhere is to be presented with the gospel on a personal level.

3. "all the nations" (Matthew 28:19, Luke 24:47): All the world's ethnic groups are intended to be reached. Jesus was telling his disciples that the task would not be complete until disciples are made of people from every ethnic grouping found on earth.

4. "to the end of the earth" (Acts 1:8): The church is responsible to carry the gospel to the far extremities from where it already exists. The end is the furthermost point one can reach from where one is presently. For a

North American, the end may be central China. For a Korean, the end may be western Europe.

5.   "to the end of the age" (Matthew 28:20): "Age" is a reference to time. The church is to continue evangelizing the world until the present age comes to an end; that end being known only to God. Lesslie Newbigin in his book *The Household of God* says this about these last two phrases:

> The Church is the pilgrim people of God. It is on the move – hastening to the ends of the earth to beseech all men to be reconciled to God, and hastening to the end of time to meet its Lord who will gather all into one...It cannot be understood rightly except in a perspective which is at once missionary and eschatological.[10]

Thus, the church is not at liberty to stop until both of these ends have been reached.

What then is the ultimate goal of the Great Commission? Bundling these five phrases together reveals where the final point of World Evangelization lies. It is the presentation of the gospel to as many people as possible, found in every people group throughout every part of the earth until this present age comes to an end.

There are some who advocate that winning just some from every people, tribe and nation (Rev. 5:9) will constitute reaching the ultimate goal of the Great Commission. However when taken together, the passages show that the task is to be ongoing and never-ending during this age. Every human being is to be sought out and given an opportunity to hear a clear presentation of the gospel until Jesus comes again (Acts 1:11).

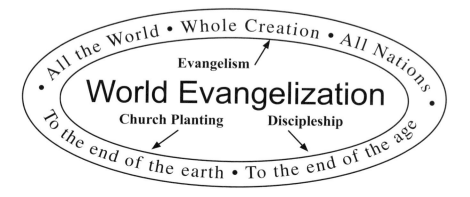

What Jesus wants you to know as you go...

There are four essential elements that make up the essence of the Great Commission. Jesus wants us to know that if the Great Commission is to be carried out properly, it will entail:

1. Worthy messengers
2. A certain message
3. A clear strategy
4. A focus on the ultimate goal

If any of these four elements are missing, then the mission could easily become either truncated or veer off course.

Borden of Yale

One bright, cultured, and wealthy young man who believed passionately in the Great Commission was William Borden. "Borden of Yale" gave millions of his fortune to the cause of world evangelization, but gave even more in the consecration of his life. As a seminary student he felt called to the unreached Muslims of Northwest China. So in 1913, renouncing the rest of his inheritance, he set sail for China to serve with the China Inland Mission. But he never made it.

His journey to China took him via Cairo to study Arabic and Islam under the well-known Islamist Samuel Zwemer. Shortly after his arrival in Egypt, he was stricken with spinal meningitis. He never recovered, and at age 25 he passed into glory.

After his death Borden's possessions were sent back to his family, which included his Bible. In it they found the words, "No Reserve" with the date placing it shortly after he had renounced his fortune in favor of missions. At a later point he had added, "No Retreat," dated at the time he was diagnosed with meningitis. Shortly before he died, as he lay ill on his hospital bed, he penned a final entry, "No Regret."

"No reserve ... no retreat ... no regret" summed up the young life of one fully devoted to Jesus' commission. Inspired by Borden's life and death, Dr. Henry W. Frost, director of the China Inland Mission, penned the following poem:

COMMISSIONED

Out from the realm of the glory-light
Into the far-away land of night;
Out of the bliss of worshipful song
Into the pain of hatred and wrong;
Out from the holy rapture above
Into the grief of rejected love;
Out from the life at the Father's side
Into the death of the crucified;
Out of high honor and into shame
The Master, willingly, gladly came:
And now, since He may not suffer anew,
As the Father sent Him, so sends He you! [12]

Chapter 8

Common Questions About the Great Commission

W e have done an in-depth study on the Great Commission teachings of Jesus. Think back over what has been accomplished thus far. First the Great Commission passages were identified; next they were synchronized; then they were analyzed; and finally, their teachings were synthesized by way of the Great Commission Diamond.

It was critical to go through these steps because of the importance of the passages to the mission of the church. Without these building blocks as a foundation, the superstructure built upon it consisting of mission principles, practices, methods and techniques would be unsound or ephemeral. Indeed, that is precisely why so many mission efforts and strategies are called into question. It is why others are woefully deficient, and why still others do not qualify as "mission" at all. They ignore the Great Commission foundation.

However, just because an exposition of the texts has been done, it doesn't mean there are not any lingering questions. Over the ages there have been good, probing questions related to the passages that demand answers. Our study would not be complete if there were not an honest attempt to deal with the more important ones.

Where are holistic ministries in the Great Commission?

With the paramount goal of the Great Commission being world evangelization (leading ultimately to the glory of God) and its strategy comprising evangelism, discipleship and planting the church (EDP), the question that naturally arises is, "Where are holistic ministries sanctioned?" Has caring for creation and the physical needs of people been ignored? Is social justice and advocating for the disenfranchised, for those in poverty, and for those with AIDS, exempt from these passages? In other words, are compassion ministries a part of them or not?

Some, who hold to a rigid interpretation of these passages, would say no. They would take the position that there is no mention anywhere in the mandates for believers to be involved in social and creation concerns as a part of the Christian mission. Others reading the same texts would respond differently. They would mention that there is indeed room for social concern in these passages if you dig deep enough. Heated discussions have ensued livening the debate as believers have grappled with the issue.

Background

In Scripture we find what are popularly referred to as two mandates; the Cultural (or social) Mandate and the Evangelistic (or gospel) Mandate. Both concepts of duty are valid and can be justified from Scripture. First, let's take the easier one. The Evangelistic Mandate, that of bringing lost souls to saving faith in Christ, is something that clearly must be carried out by God's people in obedience to the Great Commission. The first part of this book has already given an in-depth study into that mandate.

The challenge with which the Church grapples is determining what role it should play in the Cultural Mandate, and how. Should the Church's responsibility (and, perhaps, primary responsibility) be to promote social justice, provide education, engage in ecological concerns, and alleviate starvation, disease, etc? Caution needs to be exercised when answering that question. For it is important that the church on mission heed Stephen Neill's axiom, "When everything is mission, nothing is mission."[1]

It would help this discussion to put handles on what is commonly meant by the two mandates by way of precise definitions.

> **Cultural Mandate:** The qualitative and quantitative improvement of culture to benefit man and glorify God and care for creation so that man can live in a wholesome society according to moral and human rights. This

mandate was given to all mankind as members of the human race in Genesis 1:26-28; 2:15; 9:1-3.

Evangelistic Mandate: The spiritual liberation and restoration of man back into fellowship with God through repentance and forgiveness of sin. It is the restoration of God's original purpose for man, ultimately bringing him much glory. This mandate was given to believers as members of the body of Christ (Mt. 28:18-20; Mark 16:15; Lk. 24:44-48; Jn. 20:21; Acts 1:8).

The points of tension in this discussion are several. In brief, the three most common positions can be summarized as follows:

1. Some would say that the center of God's redemptive plan is to bring justice to all men everywhere. In this view the focal point is on the welfare of man, society and culture.

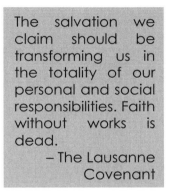

The salvation we claim should be transforming us in the totality of our personal and social responsibilities. Faith without works is dead.
    – The Lausanne Covenant

2. Others would say that the two mandates are co-equals in value; that neither is to dominate in mission. If they become dissociated, an unhealthy dichotomy arises where man is viewed only as a spiritual entity, to the neglect of physical needs and concerns.

3. Still others would argue that evangelism is paramount, because man's eternal destiny is at stake. Getting the gospel out is not only primary to the Church's mission, it is of highest priority and the only valid activity of mission.

What do the Great Commission passages have to say?

The debate is ongoing and seems to be never-ending, especially when Scripture is not consulted. It is imperative to get back to the Great Commission passages to sort out this issue. Jesus, who gave the church its mission, would of all people have something to say about this sensitive topic. And, in a subtle way he does. Three out of five of the Great Commission passages bear this out:

1. **The example of Jesus. John 20:21: "As the Father has sent me, so send I you."** In chapter 2 we learned that, in his humanity, Jesus is the prototype missionary whose life all missionaries should emulate. During

the time he was evangelistically active, Jesus was socially active as well. Out of compassion for people's physical plight (Mat.9:36) and as a means of drawing attention to his salvific message, he engaged in holistic works. Following Jesus implicitly means following his example in regard to engaging human need.

2. **The implication of Jesus. Mark 16:15: "Go into all the world and proclaim the gospel to the whole creation."** Why did Jesus use the word "creation" instead of "mankind?" Because not only is mankind affected by the fall, but also all of creation. It too is in need of redemption (Romans 8:18-23) and reconciliation (Colossians 1:19-20). Herein lies the beauty of man gaining salvation: the affects of human redemption spill over into all of the created order. When people align themselves with the Creator, a natural benefit to cultures and the environment is that they become better stewards of his creation. Eco-justice becomes a part of the church's mission through the changed hearts of those living out the gospel message. However, this reality needs to be distinguished as a by-product of what the church's mission is by command – that of evangelization.

3. **The teaching of Jesus. Matthew 28:19: "...teaching them to observe all that I have commanded you."** The "all" includes Jesus' teachings on being compassionate and performing humanitarian acts of kindness. Though many life settings and teachings of Jesus can be cited, probably the best known is his teaching in the Parable of the Good Samaritan. Certainly those specific philanthropic teaching settings must have come to mind when the disciples heard in this commission what they in turn were to teach.

A look at the Great Commission passages reveals the following distinctions:

Evangelistic Mandate	Cultural Mandate
Explicit	Implicit
Commanded by Jesus	Inferred by Jesus
Authorized by Jesus	Modeled by Jesus
Mandated to the disciples as mission	Not mandated to the disciples as mission
The goal of the Great Commission	Accompanies the Great Commission goal
Very words of Jesus	Must read between the lines
Deals with the issue of sin	Deals with the issues of society
The task	Auxiliary tasks

In summary, a study of these passages reveals that holistic ministries are implicit, not explicit in these passages, whereas evangelistic endeavors are clearly explicit. We evangelize because we are commanded to do so by Christ – this is the unequivocal mandate to believers. As such it is the primary missional task of the Church.

On the other hand, we engage in education, compassion ministries, creation care and a host of other holistic works because our new life in Christ compels us. Since we have become new creatures (2 Cor. 5:18-20), we desire that everything else in creation experience newness as well. Therefore engagement in morally right efforts like human justice and eco-justice, etc., while not a part of the church's core mission per se, become a natural by-product of or ancillary to that mission.

Mission executive Vernon Mortensen, past General Director of The Evangelical Alliance Mission (TEAM), defended the primacy of the evangelistic mandate with the following thoughtful analogy:

A hospital is a lot of things. It is a hotel where people must be housed in comfort. It is a restaurant where hundreds of meals are served daily. It is a communications center where the switchboard handles dozens of calls an hour. It is a business office where records, accounts, flow charts, and job descriptions are kept. It is a training center where doctors, nurses, and other medical personnel increase their skills.

But above all else the hospital is a place where people are healed. The purpose for its existence is the healing of the body. Therefore, central to all its varied activities is the work of the surgeon and other medical specialists. All the other activities would be pointless and futile if they did not further the skill of the medical practitioner.

Missionary work is also a lot of things. It is a combination of the skills of many trades and professions. It is a building, because houses, churches, schools, and hospitals must be built. It is linguistics, because languages must be reduced to writing, grammars and dictionaries compiled, and translations undertaken. It is medical work, because people are afflicted with a great variety of diseases which sap their strength and carry them to an early grave.

It is business administration, because finances must be cared for, personnel assigned and directed, and the work evaluated. It is relief work, because famines plague the world and natural calamities befall great numbers of people. It is education, because millions have no other opportunity of breaking out of ignorance and poverty.

But above all, its indispensable purpose is the preaching of salvation through Jesus Christ so that man's dire spiritual need may be met. It is the discipling of converts so they in turn will be able to minister to souls around them. It is the establishing of believers in spiritually effective congregations according to the New Testament pattern so there will be a living and expanding permanent witness in the community.[2]

These words are well put and worth pondering. Perhaps a good way to sum up this discussion is to consider a caution from noted missiologist George Peters:

Care must be taken, however, not to confuse the two mandates. If the two are disassociated unnaturally and unhealthily, a dichotomy arises which will work negatively upon society. If the mandates are too closely interrelated or blended, a culture-religion arises. The gospel suffers, divine priorities become blurred, and man's spiritual welfare is imperiled. The last-named is the case in the social gospel and liberalism where biblical evangelism is practically eclipsed. Evangelical social action, the social implication of the gospel, Christian service and welfare programs must remain under the judgment of the Word lest they become Christian priorities or gospel substitutes.[3]

Was the Great Commission given only for the disciples?

Believers have debated this issue for centuries. Through the ages there have been some believers who have taken the position that the Great Commission was given solely to the disciples and was something meant for them, and only them, to fulfill. This would be a convenient way to shirk responsibility for world evangelization if only it were true.

Some historical background will help bring a clear answer to this question. Coming out of the Reformation, Protestants were woefully lax in efforts to evangelize the lost. They just did not believe it to be important, and it was their narrow theological beliefs that made them so unconcerned. There were three main theological arguments that justified their inattention to it.

One was rigid predestination. In brief, this is the belief that for millions of people, salvation was neither intended nor provided by Christ. Grace was only available for a select few whom God decreed would receive it. If God decreed some to be saved, they would be saved, and if he decreed others to be damned, they would be damned. There was no grace for the spiritually condemned, since God had decreed their destruction.[4] Of course this belief deprived anyone from having any inclination to engage in the Great Commission.

Young William Carey tried to persuade the Particular Baptist, of whom he was a member and a group that held this view, that as recipients of God's grace they were obligated to use "means" to reach the unconverted. In a public meeting when he tried to convince a group of pastors of the church's responsibility, a senior colleague of his, John Ryland, squelched him with the famous lines, "Young man, sit down. When God pleases to convert the heathen then He will do it without your aid or mine."[5] (To his credit Ryland later changed his view and became a strong supporter of Carey.)

Another common belief mitigating against responsibility for the Great Commission has been the belief that the "heathen" are impossible to convert. A good example was a position taken by the Church of Scotland. At their General Assembly in 1796, they passed the declaration that, "To spread abroad among barbarians and heathen natives the knowledge of the gospel seems to be highly preposterous, in so far as it anticipates, nay even reverses the order of Nature."[6] They used the argument from Matthew 7:6, "The holy things of God are not to be cast before such dogs and swine."

Statements like that reek with colonial prejudice and naïve cultural superiority, a throwback to another era in European history. Fortunately the Scotts eventually got over that prejudice and became one of the premiere missionary sending peoples of all times. It needs to be noted that this belief also signaled a lack of faith in the power of the gospel (Romans 1:16).

Probably the most common reason why others have become indifferent to the Great Commission is the rationale that unbelievers in their own homeland should be reached first. Before thinking about going to non-believers in distant countries, those next door should be reached.[7] Increasingly, many Christ-followers in North America believe this.

This has become an even more common belief because of the acceleration of international migration that is bringing more and more foreign peoples to North America. Although this trend does demand the attention of the North American Church, there is a fatal flaw in this thinking. The truth of the matter is that we will never totally reach our own homeland no matter how intense the efforts exerted to do so. If this strategy is followed to its fullest extent, we will never get around to sending messengers outside our borders anytime soon. Consequently, we will never reach the least reached peoples in their homelands where they can in turn establish their own indigenous churches.

One last issue needs to be brought up in this regard. If believers were at liberty to pick and choose what New Testament teachings are restricted to some audiences, (like the commissions only being for the disciples), then the Bible's application would become so arbitrary that it would be left to subjectivism as to what should be obeyed.

For instance, would the fruit of the Spirit (Gal. 5:22-23) be character traits only for the Galatian believers? Would the armor of God (Eph. 6:10-18) be protection only for the Ephesian believers? Would the clothing of righteousness (Col. 3:12-14) be worn only by the Colossian believers? Of course the answer is NO on all counts! We readily apply to our lives all the other teachings of Jesus found throughout the Gospels. How can it logically follow then, that the Great Commission passages only be applied to the original hearers, and not to the rest of us as well? Obviously, a consistent hermeneutic does not permit such reasoning.

Returning to the question at hand, are the Great Commission passages applicable to Christians in all ages? The answer can only be yes. Attempts to say otherwise can be boiled down to a feeble denial of responsibility for world evangelization. Jesus will hold the Church responsible if it does not take to heart his core teaching of reaching the lost for him. If it does not, history has proven that when one sector of Christ's Church refuses to engage in the Great Commission, he raises up another sector in its place. Might this be the reason for the exponential growth of the Majority World mission movement outside of the West today?

Are these passages descriptive or prescriptive?

This question is related to the previous one when it comes to responsibility for the Great Commission. A descriptive passage is one that simply describes an event that took place with little direct application meant for the reader. A prescriptive passage, on the other hand, not only describes an event but also embeds real life principles in it that are to be followed and obeyed by all readers in all ages. Did Jesus intend for his Great Commission teachings to simply be descriptive or are they prescriptive?

Although they are located in a principally narrative section of Scripture, the narratives of the life of Jesus are always intended to teach principles that his followers in all ages are to obey. The Great Commission passages are not exempt from that intent. The Gospel writers included them for the purpose of teaching

Jesus' followers their responsibility. They prescribe in detail what the mission of Jesus is and what he wants his ambassadors to follow.

When Jesus gave the Model, Magnitude, Method, Message and Means of mission, he intended that his mission be carried out precisely as he prescribed. Granted, with the passing of time there has been some mission theory added. The core missional building blocks that he gave through each Great Commission emphasis are not to be forgotten, ignored or compromised. He precisely prescribed the essence of his mission in these passages.

Is the "Nazareth Manifesto" really at the heart of God's mission?

In recent years attempts have been made to substitute and even abrogate the Great Commission words of Jesus by other more tolerable and appealing passages. After all, Jesus surely didn't explicitly mention much about social concern and human justice in the Great Commission. So, it would be good, some would reason, to find another place that he did.

The one passage that most often stands out as the substitute for the Great Commission is what Jesus said about himself in Luke 4:18-19. Ever since James Engel and William Dyrness coaxed Christ-followers to venerate this passage above Jesus' five mission statements, uninformed believers have gravitated away from the Great Commission. The Luke passage, now commonly known as the "Nazareth Manifesto," is declared to be Jesus' personal mission statement. Therefore, the reasoning is, if it is his mission statement then it should be ours as well.

The words spoken by Jesus in Luke 4:18-19 (quoted from Isaiah 61:1-2) beautifully defined his ministry:

> "The Spirit of the Lord is upon me, because he has anointed me
> to proclaim good news to the poor. He has sent me to proclaim liberty
> to the captives and recovering of sight to the blind, to set at liberty those
> who are oppressed, to proclaim the year of the Lord's favor."

Engel and Dyrness argue that if these verses define Jesus' agenda, it follows that it must define ours also.[8] While we can grant that Jesus was concerned with physical needs, poverty, and injustice, we also know that he was more concerned with man's spiritual plight. As was noted in chapter 2, Jesus' followers are not called to perform the identical works he did. What's more, the socially slanted interpretation of these verses is not really warranted, since Jesus also describes his purpose to "proclaim good news, "and "proclaim liberty to captives," (i.e., meaning spiritual captives of the devil).

There are good reasons why the "Nazareth Manifesto" is difficult, if not impossible, for us to apply today and for it to become a legitimate substitute for the Great Commission.

- This quote by Jesus is descriptive of his mission and was not intended to be prescriptive. It describes the fulfilling of a Messianic prophecy, which can only be applied to Jesus, the true Messiah. Jesus never commanded others to do likewise, because the details were for him, and him alone, to fulfill. We dishonor his personhood when we attempt to equate our works with his.

- The passage is impossible to be carried out by every believer (if any believer at all). It contains miraculous elements that only God can perform, such as giving sight to the blind or bringing someone back to life. In contrast, the Great Commission is capable of being engaged in by every Christ-follower.

- A reading of the entire Isaiah 61 text reveals that this passage could only be applied locally – performed in and for Israel. It speaks of Zion and foreigners serving a restored Israel. These verses were not intended for universal application in all nations of the world. The geographical context does not allow it.

- All the Great Commission passages are commands of responsibility to believers. This passage is a quote and statement of fact, not a command. There are no imperatives in this text for us to obey.

- Although this passage has been called "a manifesto" (i.e., a public written declaration of principles, policies, and objectives, especially one issued by a political movement or candidate)[9], it cannot be equated with a commission. To equate them only confuses their distinctions. A manifesto makes a statement; a commission makes a demand.

To downgrade the obvious and clear-cut five Great Commission passages, and substitute them with one non-related, limited application passage is a classical hermeneutical mistake. The danger is that it leads one off track. Instead of "restoring" and "recovering a sharpened vision" of the church's mission[10] the elevation of the Nazareth Manifesto above the Great Commission passages muddies the waters and diverts the Church from its primary task. For that matter, any passage that draws us away from Jesus' Great Commission statements for any reason whatsoever should be suspect.

Since all ethnic groups have yet to be reached, does this mean Jesus cannot yet return?

Does awaiting the evangelization of all the ethnic groups in the world go counter to belief in the imminent return of Christ? If you recall, both the Matthew and Luke passages command the church to reach every ethno-linguistic group (*panta ta ethne*). There will be representatives in heaven from each of them (Rev. 5:9, 7:9, 15:3-4) and yet it is estimated that of the 16,302 groups only 9,653 have been reached. Does this mean that Jesus cannot yet return? No, it does not.

Efforts in the past

First, we do not know for certain if a people group that is not reached today had not been evangelized sometime in the past. A good example is Turkey. In past centuries the church thrived in that country. Sadly today, there are very few believers in that land. Certainly if Jesus was to return today, there will be many ethnics from Turkey in heaven, such as believers from Galatia, Colossae, and Ephesus, since the gospel was embraced there in the distant past.

Efforts in the present

Secondly, we must realize that with the migration of peoples across the globe today, we do not know if representatives from highly restricted countries containing unreached people groups have in fact been brought to Christ in the host country where they now reside. Neither do we know if there are those within unreached people blocks that, unknown to us, have been reached through media technology such as Christian radio broadcast, television, or internet. We know for a fact that there are secret believers in highly restricted places like Saudi Arabia that have found Christ through these means.

Efforts in the future

Finally, we must consider the end times. From Revelation chapter 7 we know that after God has taken the Church out of the world, he will preserve 144,000 witnesses from Israel. These witnesses, on earth during a time of great tribulation, will have the opportunity to proclaim the gospel around the globe. Theirs will be the task of "mopping up" the last remaining people groups that need to be evangelized before the final end comes.

It could well be that at this moment if Jesus were to come, there would be representatives from every people, tribe, tongue and nation gathered before his throne to praise him and thank him for his provision of salvation, though we don't know that for certain. It could be that a final ingathering will take place later by the 144,000, though we don't know that for certain either. Therefore, because of what we know from the Great Commission passages it is our responsibility to keep endeavoring to reach all peoples we know are presently unreached.

Since God at times brings unbelievers to himself through visions and dreams, is human instrumentality always necessary?

There is a fundamental flaw with this question and the reasoning behind it. The mistake is to suggest that at times God saves people through visions, dreams or other extraordinary means outside of a human witness. If that be true, then it follows that, at least at times, the Great Commission is not always applicable in winning lost humanity.

It is true that God on occasion uses unusual circumstances to get an unbeliever's attention. Accounts abound of spiritually sensitive Muslims unexpectedly seeing Jesus in dreams beckoning them to come to him, or a pre-literate tribal person encountering an angel in a vision. Seekers after God are at times rewarded by God showing himself to them in unusual ways. This can happen extraordinarily through visions, dreams, visitations by angels, or even by the more common channel of natural revelation.

However, in each of those instances, the out-of-the-ordinary revelation by God is inadequate to bring a person to saving faith in Christ. What it does do is point that person to a Christ-follower who in turn can share the gospel of Christ with him or her, resulting in that person's salvation. In every instance, that initial unusual encounter is the first step of getting the person linked to a human witness who is positioned to share the gospel with him or her. Ultimately, it takes human instrumentality to relate the necessary details for belief in Christ. That human instrumentality may come by way of a person-to-person encounter, a broadcast, printed material (including the written Scriptures), email, or any other means crafted by believers as a channel of witness.

The book of Acts bears this reality out. Zealous Saul saw a blinding light and heard the very voice of Jesus on the Damascus road, but it took Ananias to inform him of what he needed to do to be saved (Acts 9: 1-19). God-fearing Cornelius saw an angel in a vision, who spoke directly to him, but it took the person of Peter to proclaim how he was to become a follower of Jesus (Acts 10). Human witness, generated from obedience to the Great Commission, is necessary to win all men to Christ at all times.

Chapter 9

The Why of the Great Commission

For God so loved the world, that he gave his only Son, that whoever believes in him should not perish but have eternal life.
— John 3:16

S everal years ago I was flying out of central China to Beijing to catch a connecting flight to the States. Seated in the two seats next to me were a husband and wife, both of whom were on the faculty of Beijing University. They were friendly, and I could tell they were eager to use their English which, by the way, was pretty good. I had just completed a series of meetings with Christian leaders in a city of Shanxi province. Sitting there, they must have been wondering what would bring a foreigner like me to such a remote part of their country.

We engaged in typical chitchat for a while until curiosity got the better of them. They finally asked me outright why I had traveled so far from home to speak to their people and about what. I knew that as professors at a prestigious government university they could only have their positions by maintaining membership in the Communist Party. So I told them outright that I had been speaking to a group of Christians to encourage them in their faith. Intrigued, they asked what would motivate me to do such a thing? I thought about that for a moment and then responded slowly and deliberately with "because…God so loved the world, that he gave his only Son, that whoever believes in him should not perish but have eternal life." Upon hearing those words they said that they had heard them once before, during their younger years as university students in Japan, but they didn't understand their meaning.

The popularity of John 3:16

John 3:16 is considered the most popular and arguably the most recited verse of the entire Bible. It is without question the most translated piece of literature in the world. It is often the first verse memorized by new believers, or by children in Sunday school. I have seen it hanging on the walls of church nurseries and even in the palace of a King.[1] I have seen it transcribed into dozens of tribal dialects, hanging individually on plaques on the wall of a mission office on the island of Papua, signifying a Bible translation project had been undertaken in that language.

> John 3:16 is a beautiful summary of the entire gospel in fewer than 30 words. If the whole Bible had been destroyed or lost except for John 3:16, that would still be enough for any person to come to know God and to receive eternal life.
>
> – Timothy George

Most likely you have seen it in public too. You may have seen it on giant banners at football stadiums, or etched into eye smear of football players on national television.[2] Probably you have seen it on the freeway either pasted on giant billboards or whizzing by you on a car's "vanity" plate. Yes, John 3:16 is the most recognizable verse of all of Scripture.

Why is this verse so venerated among believers? Because it encapsulates the heart of the gospel like no other. The reason for the Great Commission is because of the clear-cut message of John 3:16. This one verse is a lucid summary of the entire gospel.[3] If the whole Bible were to be summed up in one verse, this would be it.[4]

The message of John 3:16 is the reason for the Great Commission. If it did not exist, neither would the Great Commission. There would be no need for it. There would be no need to go anywhere. There would be no need to make disciples. There would be no need to baptize, teach or plant churches. There would be no need to make sacrifices for Jesus, because Jesus would not have been sacrificed for us. But we know the opposite to be true. The truth of John 3:16 is a reality that happened. It is the reason for the Great Commission.

Sentimental, Not Substantive

However, I have discovered from my experiences of speaking in churches across North America that although all believers have a sentimental belief in John 3:16, many do not have a substantive belief in it. In other words, many believers can recite the verse by memory and have good feelings about it, but when quizzed about the precise meaning of what it teaches they become confused or uncertain.

Unknown to most, the greatest theological uncertainty in the minds of believers of the North American church today is the meaning of this verse. It seems that secretly, most would like to believe otherwise. Rather than affirming the exclusive message of the Cross for man's salvation, most Christians today would prefer to believe that somehow, in some way, some people, somewhere, by some other means can be saved and make it to heaven following an alternate route outside of conscious belief in the finished work of Christ. How is this manifested? By asking some probing questions about the verse that many find difficult to answer.

Five questions that come straight out of the verse will help clarify what it means. These questions are based on the words of the text itself. Red-letter edition Bibles typically mark this verse in red, signifying that Jesus spoke these words. However, others think that these words are actually from the writer John, giving his theological commentary following Jesus' encounter with Nicodemus, which ended with verse 15. Whatever the case, the verse is part of the inspired Word of God, and the question for which we need an answer remains: What would Jesus have us to know about the gospel from this one sentence? A look at the words themselves helps us discover his intent by way of the following questions.

Five probing questions related to John 3:16

1. "For God…"
   Is the God of the Bible the same god of other religions, just shrouded in different names and attributes given by humans, but in essence the same god?

This is a good place to start because so many are confused on this point. Some claim that the God who has revealed himself in the Christian Scriptures is the identical god of most every religion. It is just that Christians call him "God," whereas others call him by some other name. The Muslims call him Allah, the Hindus call him Brahman, the Buddhists call him Buddha (at least some branches do), and neo-pagans call him/her Mother Earth, Pan, Artemis or Isis, etc. So, it does not matter what god to whom you pray because in reality every deity is ultimately the same deity. Consequently, it is common to hear even believers say, "We Christians pray to the same God as the Muslims."

To hold such a belief – that of equating the God of Scripture with other gods – is to misunderstand and misrepresent God as he has revealed himself to us. It disguises who God really is and, furthermore, taints his image. It would be like being invited to the White House for a masquerade party, where everyone is asked to dress in costumes and masks to look like the President. Imagine hundreds of presidential look-alikes! Although some attendees would come very close to replicating the president and maybe even fool some into believing they were the President, there still would be only one authentic President present whom everyone else copied. When it was time for the masks to come off and the costumes to be discarded, only one genuine person, the President himself, would be left standing as the real, indisputable President of the United States who wields the authority of that office. Pretenders would be revealed for what they really were – just pretenders!

So it is with God. Although there are many pretenders, and some that are remarkably convincing counterfeits, in reality there is only one God who alone stands as the true God. This one true God is the God who has revealed himself in Scripture as the Triune God, Creator of the universe, distinct from creation but providentially in control of it. There are several ways God sets himself apart from all other gods:

a) **By his revelation**. All other religions are out to discover who god is, whereas the God of Scripture has disclosed himself to mankind. Only in the Judeo-Christian Scriptures do we find a God of revelation, who goes to great lengths to disclose himself. Our responsibility is to read and believe God's revelation about himself to gain an understanding of who he is. Nothing additional can be known about God other than what he has revealed about himself in his written word. It is left to followers then, to read, believe and personally apply his disclosure about himself to get to know God better.

Adherents of other religions have a much more difficult task. They must "discover" their god though subjective means. Some of those religions have the benefit of their "scripture" to help, but these, by their own admission, are incomplete and in need of additional discovery beyond them to better understand transcendence. Therefore, their quest leads them to seek transcendence through personal enlightenment, mystical communion, transcendental meditation, or the arbitrary word of a religious practitioner (like a mullah or a medium), to help discover their god. That is why there is such a variety of concepts of deity even within the same religion.

b) **By his exclusiveness**. God is not to be compared to any other god. He is not one god among the gods, nor the best god among all the gods. He is the only God. It grieves him deeply to be compared to a being, whether real or imagined, who is less than himself. In the Old Testament, Israel's persistent idolatry caused God to categorically declare these truths about himself:

- I am the Lord; that is my name; my glory I give to no other, nor my praise to carved idols. Isaiah 42:8

- Before me no god was formed, nor shall there be any after me. I, I am the Lord, and besides me there is no savior. Isaiah 43:10-11

- I am the first and I am the last; besides me there is no god. Isaiah 44:6

- Is there a God besides me? There is no Rock; I know not any. Isaiah 44:8

- I am the Lord, and there is no other, besides me there is no God; I equip you, though you do not know me, that people may know, from the rising of the sun and from the west, that there is none besides me; I am the Lord, and there is no other. Isaiah 45:5-6

c) **By his commandment**. God commanded that there be no rival to him, since he alone is the one true God. To believe otherwise is to violate the first command of the Ten Commandments: "You shall have no other gods before me" (Exodus 20:4). Although people being religious by nature have a concept of the divine, that concept is corrupted if it is not in agreement with what God has revealed about himself in Scripture. He commands that no other god ever be equated with him.

Just because people use religion to equate God with other gods, that is not a valid excuse for degrading God into the image man conceives him to be. German theologian Erich Saurer insightfully noted this connection with the first commandment. Writing from another era that used terminology (i.e., heathen) we shy away from today, he said this:

In his religion the heathen expresses his godlessness. Religion itself is the sin, namely the sin against the first command, the replacing of God by the gods, the most powerful expression of the opposition of man against God and contradiction within himself."[5]

So, is the God who reveals himself in Scripture the same god who is worshipped in other religions? Definitely not! "But," one may ask, "if another religion is monotheistic like Christianity is, could not their god be the same as ours?" Absolutely not! The reason this cannot be is because other monotheistic religions describe God in terms and concepts that contradict what the true and living God has revealed about himself. The god(s) of other religions are just too limited (Islam), too many (Hinduism), too human-like (new age), too transcendent (animism), or too much a figment of man's imagination (Buddhism)!

2. "…so loved the world…"
  If God is a God of love, does he not save people based on that love?

Those that raise this question hold a very common misconception of this attribute of God. Behind the question is the belief that God is so full of love that everything he does must be governed by that love. The problem with this view of God is that it makes him out to be a benevolent grandfather-type being that makes light of his high standards, which in turn contradicts his holy nature. While it is true that God by his very nature is love, that love is not an excuse for him to permit evil and sin to go unchecked in his holy presence.

If there were one attribute singled out as God's overriding attribute it would be his holiness. All of his other attributes as expressed toward man (love, justice, compassion, etc.) fall in line with and never contradict his holiness. It is sin that separates man from God and his holy presence, something that even a loving God cannot overlook. Scripture presents the issue this way:

- No person is innocent in his sin.
  "Therefore, just as sin came into the world through one man, and death through sin, and so death spread to all men because all sinned." (Romans 5:12)

- God hates sin and those that commit it.
  "The boastful shall not stand before your eyes, you hate all evildoers." (Psalm 5:5)

- Every person, as a sinful human being, is alienated from God because of that sin.

"And you, who once were alienated and hostile in mind, doing evil deeds, he has now reconciled in his body of flesh by his death, in order to present you holy and blameless and above reproach before him." (Col. 1:21-22)

- Our common sinful humanity, regardless of our religious upbringing, separates us from the holy God. Therefore, God has provided love on his terms. His great love provided a way for man to circumvent the curse of his sin and establish a relationship with him.

  "...God is love. In this the love of God was made manifest among us, that God sent his only Son into the world, so that we might live through him. In this is love, not that we have loved God but that he loved us and sent his son to be the propitiation for our sins." (I John 4:8-10)

- By his very nature God is love, but he demonstrates his love toward mankind on his terms.

  "But God shows his love for us in that while we were still sinners, Christ died for us." (Romans 5:8)

His love permitted propitiation to be made for man's sins. This was a love combined with holiness that demanded a sacrifice – not a wishy-washy automatically accept "whatever" and give-a-blanket-pardon kind of love. His holiness had to be satisfied, and out of love he satisfied it through the sacrifice of his Son. So no, he does not save people based on his love. He saves people based on his loving Provision.

3. "...that he gave his only Son..."
   If Jesus died for the world, then is not everyone already saved based on his redemptive work?

This line of thinking is rooted in a type of universalism that is sometimes called neo-universalism. Though it takes the Bible seriously and is trinitarian, it teaches that all will ultimately be saved based on Christ's provision. Its proponents believe that Jesus was indeed God and that he died for all men and purposes for all men to be saved. Therefore all will be saved by merit of Christ's death; for Christ died for all.

The difficulty with this view is that it ignores the conditional clause that follows it: "that whoever believes in him..." Every human being is responsible to make a conscious response to Christ's redeeming work. That response is belief – belief that Jesus' sacrifice was enough to satisfy God for one's personal sin.

It is true that salvation is made available to all, but it is not true that it is automatically applicable (efficacious) to all. The work of Christ demands a faith response by each individual as a show of acceptance and allegiance to Christ. Notice how many times the faith response of "believe" is mentioned in the following verse: "Whoever believes in him is not condemned, but whoever does not believe is condemned already, because he has not believed in the name of the only Son of God" (John 3:18). The human response of belief is requisite for salvation.

To put it another way, God's salvation is available to all, but only accepted by some. In theological terms, there is unlimited atonement but limited application. No, everyone is not automatically saved based on Christ's redemptive work. There is a message to be believed and a conscious response to be made.

4. "...believes in him..."
   Are there not other ways leading to God besides solely through Jesus Christ?

To discredit the uniqueness of Jesus has been the quest of every major religion since the days he walked this earth. Judaism and Islam seem to be the most intent on doing this, but neo-paganism and others, like new-age spiritualists, are not far behind. The goal of discrediting Jesus' uniqueness is also to discredit his unique redemptive work.

Certainly, some suggest, there must be alternative ways leading to God other than through the exclusive work of Jesus Christ. How can there possibly be only one way? After all, they contend, does not that position smack of elitism, privilege and even spiritual bigotry? Would not the Hindu scriptures be more palatable that say, "howsoever man may approach me, even so do I accept them; for on all sides, whatever path they may choose is mine" (Bhagavad-Gita, iv.11)?

There are many today who prefer to customize their religious beliefs, drawing from a smorgasbord of religious options. For them it is not a matter of choosing one path, but the mixing of several paths. To eclectically choose from an assortment of beliefs in order to personalize one's own beliefs is in vogue and a sign of intelligent "spirituality."

One of the most influential persons in America does just that and uses her extremely popular clout to influence many others to do the same. Oprah Winfrey, a spiritual "advisor" for many, is a prime representative of this popular spirituality. Drawing from Christianity, Judaism, Buddhism and other religions, she has set the course by saying, "One of the biggest mistakes humans make is to believe there is only one way. Actually there are many diverse ways leading to what you call 'God.'"[6]

The Apostle Peter said something much different. Standing before a group of distinguished religious scholars he said, "There is salvation in no one else, for there is no other name under heaven given among men by which we must be saved" (Acts 4:12). Previously, as a disciple, Peter had heard Jesus proclaim, "I am the way, and the truth, and the life. No one comes to the Father except through me" (John 14:6). Peter now elaborates on that declaration made by Jesus by saying two things that are helpful to those who have an inkling that somehow, somewhere, some other people, by some other means can come to God.

First, he says that geographically, no matter where one may go on this earth, whether it be deep into the jungles of the Amazon basin or to the top of the Himalayas, there are no people located anywhere "under heaven" that have discovered another name whereby they can be saved. The persistent romantic belief that somewhere in the distant reaches of the earth others may have found a way to gain acceptance by God through another means other than through Jesus Christ is not plausible.

Second, looking at the issue another way, Peter says there is neither any group of people nor ethnic group of humanity ("given among mankind") that has discovered salvation apart from Christ. Whether the Batak of Sumatra or the Belgians of Europe, no people group has discovered a way to have a right relationship with God within themselves. Anthropologists tell us that there are about 16,000 ethnolinguistic people groups in the world. Peter says that not one of them, even though they be many (so the chances are great), has discovered salvation outside of belief in Christ.

These two phrases press the claim of the universal need for Jesus to the fullest extent.[7] Salvation is found in Christ alone. All peoples, no matter where they reside or what belief system they hold, must "believe in him." So, to answer the question at hand: no, there are no other ways leading to God besides through Jesus Christ. He alone can save.

5. "...should not perish but have eternal life."
Aren't non-believers annihilated or simply "extinguished" at death?

Though a quick reading of this verse may make it look like at the time of death some (unbelievers) are annihilated whereas others (believers) keep living forever, this is not what the end of the verse is saying. The word translated "perish" (*apolumi*) can just as readily be translated "separated" or "set apart." Those who die without believing in Jesus will perish in the sense that they will be separated from God. Their destiny is not obliteration, but rather a ruin of continued existence outside of God's presence forever.

The thought of such a destiny is both sobering and heart wrenching. Believers never take pleasure in the condemnation of the lost, no matter how bad the person might have been in this life. Divine retribution is a terrible thing – something that all deserve, but all want to avoid because just as eternal life is everlasting, so eternal separation is everlasting as well.

For some theologians, the thought of nonbelievers experiencing eternal conscious punishment is intolerable.[8] They believe the verse teaches that although the reward for belief is eternal life, the punishment for unbelief is eternal annihilation. For them God does not raise the wicked in order to consciously torture them forever, but rather to declare his judgment upon them and then condemn them to extinction, which is the second death.[9]

However, there are many passages in Scriptures that say otherwise. Of all people, Jesus had more to say about hell as a place of eternal conscious punishment than anyone else (Mat. 3:12; 18:8; 25:41,46; Mk. 9:43-48). To help drive home his point, he gave a sobering parable about the rich man and Lazarus (Luke 16:19-31). From that parable six realities about death are evident:

1) There is continued existence after physical death.
2) There is a separate destiny for believers and nonbelievers.
3) That destiny is final.
4) The decision is made in this life as to where one spends eternity.
5) People cannot transfer from one place of destiny to another – the location is irrevocably set at the time of death.
6) Once in hell a person cannot send a messenger to warn loved ones – it is too late for that to be done. Loved ones must be informed and warned by the living.

Wrapping it up

The following statement summarizes what this verse and other Scripture are teaching in regard to salvation: Salvation is found in no one else, but is based solely on the merits of the historic finished work of the sinless Christ on the cross on behalf of sinful mankind. One must consciously place his faith (trust) in Christ's redemptive work and thus experience a personal conversion in order to be saved.

This summary takes the following set of beliefs into account:

- All humans are sinners, by nature and by choice, and are therefore guilty and under divine condemnation.
- Salvation is only through Christ and his atoning work.
- Belief is necessary to obtain the salvation achieved by Christ. Therefore the church has a responsibility to tell unbelievers the good news about Jesus Christ.
- Adherents of other religions, no matter how sincere their belief or how intense their religious activity, are spiritually lost apart from God.
- Physical death brings to an end the opportunity to exercise saving faith and accept Jesus Christ. The decisions made in this life are irrevocably fixed at death.
- At the great final judgment, all humans will be separated on the basis of their relationship to Christ during this life. Those who have believed in him will spend eternity in heaven, in everlasting joy and reward in God's presence. Those who have not accepted him will experience hell, a place of unending suffering, where they will be eternally separated from God.[10]

The following is a simple story to help illustrate the importance of John 3:16 to the Great Commission.

The Mouse Trap
(Author Unknown)

A mouse looked through the crack in the wall to see a farmer open a package.

"What food might this contain?" the mouse wondered. He was devastated to discover it was a mousetrap. Retreating to the farmyard, the mouse proclaimed the warning: "There is a mousetrap in the house! There is a mousetrap in the house!"

The chicken clucked and scratched, raised her head and said, "Mr. Mouse, I can tell this is a grave concern to you, but it is of no consequence to me. I cannot be bothered by it."

The mouse turned to the pig and told him, "There is a mousetrap in the house! There is a mousetrap in the house!" The pig sympathized, but said, "I am so very sorry, Mr. Mouse, but there is nothing I can do about it but pray. Be assured you are in my prayers."

The mouse turned to the cow and said "There is a mousetrap in the house! There is a mousetrap in the house!" The cow said, "Wow, Mr. Mouse. I'm sorry for you, but it's no skin off my nose."

So, the mouse returned to the house, head down and dejected, to face the farmer's mousetrap alone.

That very night a sound was heard throughout the house – like the sound of a mousetrap catching its prey. The farmer's wife rushed to see what was caught. In the darkness, she did not see it was a venomous snake whose tail the trap had caught. The snake bit the farmer's wife. The farmer rushed her back to bed, but she began to get hot with fever.

Everyone knows you treat a fever with fresh chicken soup, so the farmer took his hatchet to the farmyard for the soup's main ingredient. But his wife's sickness continued, so friends and neighbors came to sit with her around the clock. To feed them, the farmer went out to the barn yard and butchered the pig.

The farmer's wife did not get well; she died. So many people came for her funeral; the farmer had the cow slaughtered to provide enough meat for all of them. The mouse looked upon it all from his crack in the wall with great sadness.[11]

What's the moral as it relates to this discussion? Simply this: John 3:16 is at the core of all of Christian theology. We must beware lest, like the "harmless" mousetrap, it is ignored, denied, or considered of little consequence. It is at the center of God's redemptive plan. To deny it is to threaten all of Christian theology.[12] To ignore it is, by implication, to also ignore the importance of the Great Commission.

What Jesus wants you to know as you go...

John 3:16 is both the logical and theological reason for the Great Commission. This one verse explains the source of salvation (God); his motive for granting salvation (love); the object of his salvation (the world); his provision of salvation (his only Son); the way to appropriate salvation (believe in him); and the eternal benefit of salvation (not perish but have eternal life). The entire gospel is encapsulated in this one verse.

Chapter 10

Leadership Principles from the Great Commission

It is not difficult to think of Jesus as a master teacher. But how often do we think of him as a masterful leader? Unquestionably he was that and more. He was the consummate leader who perfectly balanced leadership skills and practices, which impacted the lives of many. Over time his magnetic persona and mighty acts, coupled with his leadership skills, were so effective that they caused a following of men and women to bond together, who he knew had the potential of advancing a mission that would literally change the world.

He knew however that the success of this mission would not be automatic. Jesus understood that capable leaders were crucial to its success. If the overarching goal of world evangelism was to be achieved, then much was dependent upon the abilities of responsible men and women who were capable of positively influencing others. Good leadership on their part would play a large part in attaining desired results. As someone has said, "leadership is the cause, everything else is the effect."

So by intent, Jesus masterfully wove leadership principles throughout his Great Commission statements. These principles were designed not only to be caught by the eleven, but by succeeding generations of believers after them – right down to us! Take a look at the following leadership principles. They are important for followers of Jesus to know and apply as they go on mission.

Foundational Mission Leadership

Let's start with a very basic question: what makes mission leadership distinctly "mission?" Or put another way, what are the marks of a good mission leader? These questions are important and demand some reflection. Before trying to answer, it would be wise to take a step back and nail down what are the fundamental marks of a good *Christian* leader. For, a good *mission leader* must first and foremost exhibit the traits of a good *Christian leader*.

Jesus, in one of his better-known parables, best summed up the traits of a good Christian leader. In the "Parable of the Talents," he spoke of a master (portraying God the Father) commending a servant with the words, "well done my good and faithful servant" (Mt. 25:23). From that brief commendation it can be deduced that good Christian leadership involves excellence in performance ("well done"), excellence in character ("good"), excellence in fidelity ("faithful"), and excellence in serving others ("servant").

It is imperative that mission leaders exhibit these Christian leadership marks. However, in whatever level of mission leadership one is engaged; whether it be as an in-the-trenches project director, a team leader, a field director, a regional supervisor, a home office middle manager, a mission vice-president, or a CEO, all must exercise something that goes beyond the four fundamental Christian leadership traits. Mission leaders must exhibit these Christian leadership marks. However, there is something else uniquely related to mission that must be added if leadership is to be characterized as distinctly "mission leadership."

In order to realize that distinction, one must recall that our English word "mission" is derived from the Latin *mitto*, which in turn is a translation of the Greek word "apostle" or "sent one." Therefore, the additional responsibility incumbent on ALL mission leaders is the promoting of what distinctly pertains to the Church's outreach to the world. A heart for, and a deliberate focus on, the organized and intentional dissemination of the gospel as it is taken from where it is known and believed to where it is not known or believed, is the quality that distinguishes one as a mission leader. This added responsibility is something Jesus passed on when he gave the Great Commission instruction to his disciples. Four threads run through these passages that highlight what is included in this leadership trait that makes it distinctively mission.

These threads align with the four basic components that comprise any "mission" as noted by David Bosch.[1] In chapter 2 it was noted that Bosch observed that in essence a mission, whether it be diplomatic, business or religious must entail: 1) a sender, 2) the one sent, 3) those to whom one is sent (audience), and 4) an assignment. Leadership that distinctly pertains to mission, especially Christian mission, encompasses these four components – all of which were mentioned by Jesus.

Mission leadership and the sender

A mission leader is one who is authorized by God the Father to go (Mt. 28:18), is sent by the Son (Jn. 20:21), and empowered by the Holy Spirit (Acts 1:8). He is aware of that special calling which drives him to leave his native environ on assignment for Christ. He has the authoritative audacity to so go. He has no doubt about the importance of the divine directive that he is obeying, which is coupled with supernatural enabling (Acts 1:8). Together, these compel him to unapologetically, yet with sensitivity, cross over into other communities, countries, continents, and cultures so the gospel is propagated.

Mission leadership and the messenger

A mission leader is first and foremost himself a messenger, as well as a facilitator of other messengers. His life models that of Christ (Jn. 20:21) and his voice proclaims the gospel (Mk. 16:15). A mission leader knows and believes beyond a shadow of a doubt the importance of the message he proclaims. He understands that the root problem of mankind is sin, of which all peoples everywhere need forgiveness in order to be restored to a right relationship with God. He understands that repentance is the necessary response for anyone, located anywhere, living in any culture, to be accepted by God (Lk. 24: 46).

Mission leadership and the audience

The audience are those to whom a messenger is sent. The mission leader understands that the magnanimity of God's redemptive act has a universal appeal that is designed to be available to all peoples everywhere. The mission leader also notes that Jesus gave at least three metrics to employ when measuring how far the task has progressed before it can be considered completed:

- The individual metric: the gospel proclaimed until every human being has had an opportunity to clearly hear its presentation (Mk. 16:15, "all creatures").
- The ethnical metric: the gospel penetrating into every distinct ethnic group found on earth (Mt. 28:19, Lk. 26:47, "all peoples").

- The geographical metric: the gospel carried forth from Jerusalem to Judea and Samaria until it reaches the remotest parts of the earth (Acts 1:8, Mk 16:15, "all the world").

Mission leadership and the assignment

Although there are a plethora, and innumerable variety, of tasks that missionaries perform, the mission leader understands that the centerpiece of the mission endeavor is to "make disciples." This is accomplished as missionaries go, baptize, and teach (Mt. 28:19). Mission leaders understand that the validity of all auxiliary mission enterprises – whether social concern, support ministries, humanitarian work, or relief and development – supplement the core assignment of making disciples, which normally culminates in the establishment of maturing churches. To that end, no matter what a missionary's specific assignment, it should entail witness (Acts 1:8) and proclamation (Mk. 16:15).

To return to the original question: what comprises leadership that is distinctively "mission" in nature? It would seem that no matter what level of mission leadership one is engaged, the four components mentioned above are essential. A "Great Commission" understanding of the sender, the messenger, the audience and the assignment are the foundation on which all other mission leadership theory, skills and practices are built. This comprises leadership that is uniquely missional. This is leadership upon which global outreach is centered.

Jesus' Leadership Challenge

In their classic book *The Leadership Challenge*, James Kouzes and Barry Posner unpack five leadership practices common to personal-best leadership experiences. These best practices are based on extensive research. It is uncanny to note that two thousand years before their study, Jesus touched on these identical leadership principles within his Great Commission statements. Take a look at the leadership practices delineated by Kouzes and Posner and then note how Jesus tied them into the post-resurrection instruction to his disciples.

1. Leadership Practice #1: Modeling the Way
   Good leaders model the behavior they expect of others, especially their followers.

Jesus' instruction: "As the Father has sent me, even so I am sending you." (Jn. 20:21)

In chapter 2 it was noted that, by way of his life and ministry, Jesus set the standard for service. He modeled how his followers are to conduct themselves while engaged in the task of carrying the gospel to the world. His life has become the standard for everything: character, morals, ethical behavior and performance. It was noted that by emulating his life, no follower of Jesus will ever need to question whether his conduct is consistent with the gospel he proclaims.

> If you don't believe in the messenger, you won't believe the message.
> – Kouzes & Posner

The two conjunctions "As...so" show by comparison how one can duplicate Jesus' lifestyle in personal conduct and public ministry. The solemn teaching of Jesus is that his messengers are to manifest his life and character in their ministries. Just as Jesus manifested the character of God in his environment of influence, so believers are to bear that same kind of witness as they minister in theirs.

2. Leadership Practice #2: Inspire a Shared Vision
   Leaders see attractive opportunities and imagine possibilities. They then enlist others by breathing life into their hopes and dreams, enabling them to envision exciting future possibilities as well.

Jesus' instruction: "Go into all the world and proclaim the gospel to the whole creation." (Mk. 16:15)

In chapter 3 it was noted that Jesus used two phrases to show the disciples the magnitude of the task: "into all the world" and "to the whole creation." Their minds must have reeled as they contemplated the shared vision Jesus was inspiring in them! Jesus had said some challenging things to them in the past, but now their new mission was to include a vision that encompassed the entire world, to the whole of creation. Their endeavor was not to be limited to national, regional or even empire-wide boundaries. It was to include the entire earth – global in proportion! How much grander can a vision be than that!

3. Leadership Practice #3: Challenge the Process
   Leaders challenge the status quo and pioneer innovative new products, programs and procedures.

Jesus' instruction: "Go therefore and make disciples of all nations, baptizing them in the name of the Father and of the Son and of the Holy Spirit, teaching them to observe all that I have commanded you." (Mt. 28:19-20)

How did Jesus follow this practice? First, he challenged the prevailing view of the time, that non-Jews were to make their way to the land of Israel to worship the true and living God. Now that process was to be reversed. Instead of centering their witness in Jerusalem and waiting upon the nations to be drawn to them, they were to "go," starting from Jerusalem, and fan out across the Roman Empire and beyond. They were to engage in a new centrifugal, outward mission. This thrusting forth from Jerusalem constituted a challenge to and change of prevailing Jewish missional tactics.

Second, Jesus instituted an innovative new procedure for the success of world evangelization. The "making of disciples" entailed much more than the normative procedure of proselytizing. The former involves life-changing transformation; the latter usually involves only a change in religious allegiance. The outcome sought is to have genuine conversions to Christ rather than shallow nominalism, which is all too typical.

4. Leadership Practice #4: Enable Others to Act
   The good leader knows that leadership is a team effort built on good relationships. In an atmosphere of trust he empowers others to feel capable and to achieve their highest potential.

Jesus' instruction: "And behold, I am sending the promise of my Father upon you. But stay in the city until you are clothed with power from on high." (Lk. 24:49) "But you will receive power when the Holy Spirit has come upon you..." (Acts 1:8).

Jesus told the disciples not to go anywhere until they first were properly empowered. He could not overemphasize the importance of this supernatural empowerment. As was mentioned in chapter 6, the work of missions can only be effectively carried out through the supernatural enablement of the Holy Spirit. Only he can empower and energize believers for the task that in every respect is far too daunting and dangerous for them to accomplish on their own.

The disciples knew they would be at a disadvantage without Jesus physically present by their side. It was an assurance to them, therefore, to know that another divine member of the Trinity would be with them and empower them to do what they could not do in and of themselves. By his power they would have both the courage and empowerment to be Christ's ambassadors.

5. Leadership Practice #5: Encourage the Heart

A good leader shows genuine acts of caring. He visibly and behaviorally links rewards with performance, building a strong sense of collective identity.

Jesus' instruction: "And behold, I am with you always, to the end of the age." (Mt. 28:20)

Jesus didn't mention much about rewards for performance in the Great Commission passages. Maybe he didn't want that to be the overriding motivation factor for some as they engaged in mission. However, he did have something to say about caring for those who do carry out his mission. Jesus promised to go with each of the eleven as they in turn went on their mission outreaches.

Although the impact of this promise was not realized at the moment, what a comfort it must have been to the disciples after they scattered across the globe to reflect on it. It is reassuring to know that Jesus is with his messengers at all times in every age. His ongoing presence is promised right through to the end of time. There is no place they will go where he will not be present, no time when he will be absent. The omnipresent and eternal nature of Jesus guarantees this promise forever to be true.

Modeling the way, inspiring a shared vision, challenging the process, enabling others to act, and encouraging the heart, were all part of the leadership style of Jesus. Then he made sure the leaders of this new movement knew about them as well. These basic leadership practices would help assure success in the ongoing propagation of the gospel.

Leadership Succession Principles: Passing the Baton

In covering the 2008 Beijing Olympics for Yahoo Sports, Josh Peter wrote, "If they awarded medals for ineptitude, the U.S. track team would have won the gold." He was referring to the disastrous 4x100 relay races in which both the men's and the women's teams failed to advance because of dropping the baton during the exchange.[2]

Just before Jesus ascended into heaven, he said that his work on earth was complete. Passing the baton to his disciples, he declared that they were next in line to go into all the world and bring good news to the nations. He perfectly modeled the process of leadership transition to them. Succession planning was important to the success of their mission, and he knew he had to include important elements in his farewell addresses that would help them succeed.

The business world understands the importance of successful leadership transition, especially as it relates to the succession of the top leaders. Frances Hesselbein, the former CEO of the Drucker Foundation for Nonprofit Management, has said this about leadership transition: "Few events in the life of an organization are as critical, as visible, or as stressful as when the leader leaves the organization. Effective leaders plan an exit that is as positive and graceful as their entrance was."[3]

It is the responsibility of the leader to plan, communicate and coordinate the period of leadership transition.[4] Jesus did this perfectly with his disciples. At his post-resurrection meetings with them he informed, inspired, mobilized and motivated them for a future of service without him. He didn't just abandon them, leaving them in a lurch to figure it all out on their own.

Principles of successful succession are evident throughout the Great Commission passages. A competent departing leader ensures that at the very least the basic grounding principles of the movement or organization are in place and understood by his successors. Jesus ensured that the following three were understood:

- A Mission statement. A defined mission gives reason and meaning for existence and thus motivates successors. Jesus gave his disciples a precise and concise mission that boiled down to five words: "make disciples of all nations" (Mt. 28:19).

- A Vision statement. A clarified vision gives inspiration to successors for sacrificial service. Jesus passed along to his disciples a clear, inspiring, and vast vision: "Go into all the world and proclaim the gospel to the whole creation" (Mk 16:15).

- Authority to act. Authority gives confidence to successors to act and move forward. Jesus assured the disciples that they had the right given from heaven itself to do what he was asking of them: "All authority in heaven and on earth has been given to me" (Mt. 28:18). He then commands them to go based on that authority.

These three essential elements are critical in any leadership transition. Jesus was well aware of that and made sure they were included in his final instructions. The disciples' success in his absence depended upon them grasping the importance of each.

Who's THE new leader?

In this particular setting of leadership transition, the question arises, "Why didn't Jesus appoint one of the twelve to succeed him as their leader before he left them?" Would it not have been advantageous and even organizationally prudent that one of them be appointed the new leader with authority over the others?

The answer to that question is found in the nature of their task. They were each being sent elsewhere on mission. They were not to band together and form a center of operation that would morph into an organization that in turn would demand officers and structure. Rather, they were pioneers of a movement – a movement that did not need centralization. The plan was for each of them to spread out across the world on travels that would take them hundreds if not thousands of miles apart from each other. They didn't need a singular leader. Instead each of them would be just as important as the other.

Nor did they need a common center. Each of them would pioneer centers of their own elsewhere. To facilitate its rapid spread, the Church was not to have one, but many centers. They were to start from Jerusalem (Luke 24:49), and then fan out to every point of the compass, making the Church multi-centric. While it is true that different centers would belong to a single organism, it would not have a single organizational structure. Centralization would have only hampered their mission, not helped it. Thus there was no need for one major leader or a common center.

Running with the baton: the apostles on mission

After Jesus ascended into heaven his eleven companions were never again called "disciples." They had graduated from learners to heralders. They were now officially "apostles," or "sent ones." As amazing as it seems, not one of them abandoned the cause or their calling. Not one of them defected, backslid, refused to go, or reverted to his previous profession. Jesus successfully ingrained the importance of the Great Commission so deeply into their hearts that it became their burning passion until their deaths.

We don't find much in the Scriptures about the missionary activities of the eleven apostles. We are left to leaf through the annals of history and church tradition to discover where they served and how far they went. Although at times the reliability as to the details of these accounts are questioned, nevertheless they do serve as a guide. They give us a rather dependable picture of where these men went, what they accomplished, and how they died.

The following are their stories. Their life summaries are mentioned in the order that their names are listed by Luke in Acts 1:13.[5]

Peter

Peter spent his first years working among the Jews in Jerusalem and throughout Judea. As the apostle who held the "keys" of opening doors to the gospel (Mt. 16:17-19), he boldly opened the door to the Jews (Acts 2), the Samaritans (Acts 8), and the Gentiles (Acts 10). Eventually he went to Rome, where it is traditionally believed he became the first bishop. He may have been executed during the persecutions under Emperor Nero in AD 64, or later in AD 67. That being the case, we can calculate that he gave at least 34 years to missionary service. He authored 1 and 2 Peter, and heavily influenced the content of the Gospel of Mark. Tradition says Peter was crucified upside down in Rome.

John, younger brother of James

John was probably the only disciple who died a natural death. After ministry in Jerusalem, sometime later he went to western Asia Minor (Turkey). He became bishop of Ephesus, south of Izmir, influencing the churches scattered around Asia Minor. During the reign of Domitian (AD 81-96), as an elderly man he was banished to the island of Patmos in the Aegean Sea. He was later freed and died a very old man in Ephesus. He was the most prolific writer among the Apostles, authoring the Gospel of John, 1,2,3 John and Revelation. The early church recognized him as "John the theologian."

James, son of Zebedee

James seems to have ministered in and around the city of Jerusalem for over a decade. He stayed in the area of Judea, focusing on his own people, the Jews. His success must have caused great consternation among the Jewish leadership because fourteen years into his ministry they orchestrated his arrest and execution. He was martyred (beheaded) by being "put to the sword" (Acts 12:1-2) under a persecution by Herod Agrippa I in AD 44. He was the first of the Apostles to die.

Andrew, the brother of Peter

There are credible claims that Andrew went off to Achaia (southern Greece) and then pioneered missions into Scythia (Ukraine and southern Russia). Because of his activities, centuries later he was declared the patron saint of Russia. Returning to Greece, he was crucified at Patras in Achia. A later tradition describes him as being crucified in a spread-eagle position. Centuries later his relics were taken to Scotland, where the Scots were introduced to the gospel. Thus the origin of St.

Andrew's cross of Scotland. When the Union Jack was designed, St. Andrew's cross was placed on the bottom.

Philip

Philip became a missionary to west-central Asia Minor (Turkey). He ministered in the area of Hieropolis and nearby Colossae and Laodicea. It seems he was martyred there, but the records are sketchy as to how or when. Polycrates, bishop of Ephesus during the second century, mentions Philip as, "one of the twelve who lived as one of the great lights of Asia and is buried at Hieropolis with his two aged daughters."

Thomas (Didymus)

"Doubting Thomas" became "Determined Thomas." Not long after Jesus' ascension, Thomas began to make his way eastward. He traveled further and wider than any of the other Apostles. According to church tradition, Thomas crossed countries, kingdoms, continents, rivers and into diverse religious communities to herald the gospel. He did not stop until he reached the most extreme parts of the earth then known to man. He kept on going until he made his way to what is today southern India, a remarkable journey for that day! There he died a martyr's death, and that is probably the only thing that kept him from going even further. It is believed he was speared to death near the city of Madras on the east coast. Mount St. Thomas, near Madras and the Indian Mar Thomas Church is associated with him.

Bartholomew, also known as Nathanael

The missionary work of Bartholomew (Nathanael) is linked with Armenia (present day Armenia in eastern Turkey, northern Iraq and northwestern Iran). He must have ministered in this area for quite a few years. It has been said that he met death by being skinned alive and then beheaded. Traditionally the city of Derbent, north of present day Baku on the western shores of the Caspian Sea has been recognized as his place of martyrdom.

Matthew, also known as Levi

Early Church leaders tell us that Matthew became an apostle to the Jews. His Gospel is written to Jews with Jewish references permeating it. It abounds with quotations from the Old Testament, as he wants his readers to acknowledge Jesus as the Jewish Messiah. This is likely why it was placed as the first book of the New Testament – to transition from the Old Testament to the New. According to tradition he took his missionary work south of Israel into Ethiopia. It is believed he died as a martyr there after a career of more than 30 years.

James, son of Alphaeus

This second James is usually designated as "James the Less" to distinguish him from James the son of Zebedee. This is because we know so little about him and of his importance to church history as we know it. Tradition claims that James first ministered in Palestine among the Jews, and then went to Egypt. It is believed he was martyred there, but there are only scant details of his death or ministry there.

Simon the Zealot (or Patriot)

For a man known as a patriot, leaving his homeland took some doing. But that is exactly what Simon was willing to do for the cause of Christ. We know he was an ardent patriot because he is labeled as such in every list. It must have been a status he was proud of and made sure others knew about. But something changed him. Instead of being zealous for his party and homeland, he became zealous for the Kingdom of God. He was moved to give his life for the cause of Christ rather than for the cause of his country. Tradition says that he joined up with Judas in Persia and ministered with him there. He too was martyred, possibly hacked to death.

Judas, son of James (also known as Thaddaeus)

This Judas is not to be confused with Judas Iscariot who betrayed Jesus, nor with Jude one of the brothers of Jesus who wrote the New Testament book of Jude. Records are very sketchy about his missionary activity. It is believed that he went east, first to Assyria (eastern Iraq), then to Persia (Iran) before joining up with Simon the Zealot in Persia and being killed with him there.

Running with the baton: our turn

The extraordinary missionary careers of each of the Apostles show how strongly they believed in the cause of Jesus' commission to them. No other group of men has been so dedicated to a pioneering movement as they were. Their steadfast devotion to the task with which Jesus commissioned them was beyond remarkable. They spearheaded a movement that truly "turned the world upside down" (Acts 17:6).

In the sport of track, dropping the baton is the major mistake a relay team can make that would cause the team to fall far behind the other runners and most certainly lose the race. If any runner on the four-person team drops the baton as she is running, she must stop and pick it up before continuing her "leg" of the run. Why? Because it is required that the final runner on the team cross the finish line with baton in hand.

The apostles did not "drop the baton" of world evangelization. Once filled with the Holy Spirit, each of them shot "out of the blocks" running and did not let up until he had finished his leg of the race. With the gospel baton in hand they carried it the first leg of the journey to the world. After their segment of the race was run, they handed it off to the next generation, and the next generation passed it off to the next and the next did the same until this present age.

Where the Apostles Served and Died

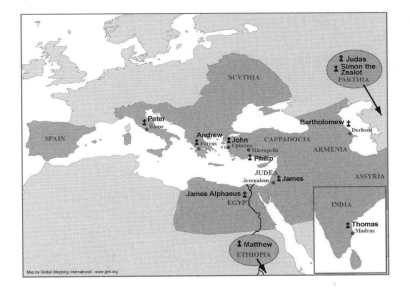

Map by Global Mapping International - www.gmi.org

Conclusion

If there be any one summary that best describes the spirit, motivation and drive of these eleven men as they went about their task, it would be by mission writer J. Herbert Kane:

> To this end the King has given orders to His ambassadors. They are to go into all the world, preach the gospel to every creature, and make disciples of all nations (Mt 28:19). All men everywhere are required to repent and believe the gospel (Acts 17:30). Only by so doing can they be delivered from the dominion of darkness and be transferred to the kingdom of light (Co 1:13). Nothing short of world conquest is the ultimate goal, and the King has given assurance that one day the kingdoms of this world are to become the Kingdom of our Lord and of His Christ (Re 11:15). There is no ambiguity about the plan, no uncertainty about the outcome.

Jesus shall reign where'er the sun
Doth its successive journeys run;
His kingdom spread from shore to shore
Till moons shall wax and wane no more.

Chapter 11

The Remaining Task

S ince the Day of Pentecost, devoted followers of Christ have been avidly taking the message of the gospel across continents, countries and cultures. Yet after 2000 years, the quest to fulfill Christ's commission has gone uncompleted. This is true even though there has been no greater effort in the history of mankind that compares in scope and expenditure to this undertaking. Literally hundreds of thousands of messengers have gone forth, billions of dollars expended, and innumerable prayers offered on its behalf. Over the centuries hundreds of vibrant regional sending centers emerged and then disappeared as zeal for mission waxed and waned. Through it all, the propagation of the gospel has continued unbroken and unabated. Sadly however, the task still remains uncompleted.

What's more, messengers have been sent out from every race and peoples imaginable. Some have had distinguished and remarkable careers. Others, who comprise the vast majority of the force, have served quietly and over time have been lost to history. Many have served with distinction, whereas some fell into disgrace. Most, through self-denial, gave up much only to see very few results in return. But this much can be said of all: that they served in obedience to the call of Christ on their lives based on his Great Commission.

One would expect that with so many engaged in this endeavor over so many centuries, that the task would be close to completion. Regrettably, that is not the case. Although remarkable progress has been made on some fronts, the vast majority of the world's peoples remain unevangelized. The task of winning the world for Christ still looms large and incomplete as the Church enters the second decade of this third millennium.

How can it be determined what still remains to be done? By looking at the remaining task from several different perspectives and employing certain metrics mentioned in the Great Commission passages themselves, we can know the present state of world evangelization.

The comparative perspective

The following table helps us understand how mankind is grouped according to religions. Some clarification is necessary to fully understand these statistics.[1] Christianity is by far the largest religion of the world. Not only that, it continues to experience phenomenal growth around the globe. It is the only religion that is strongly global. Each of the three largest religions – Christianity, Islam and Hinduism – are growing faster than the world population. However, Islam and Hinduism can attribute the majority of their growth to large birth rates in their strongest spheres. This is known as biological growth.

Christianity, on the other hand, not only has a strong biological growth rate, but its evangelical sector has an annual growth rate of 2.11%, making it the fastest growing religion through the more important category "conversion growth." Since most growth is occurring in the Majority World, it is making for the shrinking of Christianity in the Western hemisphere, and conversely for exponential growth in the Southern hemisphere.[2] The center of gravity of Christianity is no longer "north" as it had been for centuries. It has progressively gravitated southward over the past decades so that now it has become centered in the "south."

Interestingly, over the past 100 years, adherents to Christianity have maintained 33% of the total world population. Some project that with the Church now fully centered "South" in the Majority World, where population growth rates are high, Christianity will begin to see an even larger margin of percent of the total population in the decades to come.

Status of World Religions Today[2]

	Adherents 2010	Growth in %	Estimate for 2025
World Population	6,900,000,000	1.22	8,010,511,000
Christian	2,275,727,000	1.32	2,714,741,000
Muslims	1,451,614,000	1.75	1,880,731,000
Hindus	915,455,000	1.35	1,090,008,000
Non-Religious	775,947,000	0.14	819,374,000
Chinese	388,609,000	0.64	425,919,000
Buddhists	387,872,000	0.73	438,079,000
Tribal Religions	266,281,000	1.01	287,041,000
Atheists	148,350,000	0.22	149,110,000
New Religions	106,183,000	0.55	110,814,000
Sikhs	23,990,000	1.51	29,483,000
Jews	15,088,000	0.80	16,779,000

Of course, a critical question is what percentage of those who are labeled "Christian" are true followers of Jesus Christ? Another term frequently used for true Christ-followers is "Great Commission Christians." Great Commission Christians are those who believe:

- The Bible as God's unique revelation to man, that is both truthful and trustworthy in all that it says from start to finish.
- Jesus to be the unique incarnation of God, who is fully God and fully man, who lived a sinless and perfect life on earth, qualifying him to become the Redeemer of mankind.
- Salvation is only through the person and work of Jesus Christ when he died an atoning death on the cross for mankind; something a person must personally believe and accept in this life.
- Intentional witness must be proclaimed to the lost, as a means of bringing them to faith in Christ.[3]

Sadly, only a small percentage of those who are labeled as "Christian" in the statistics above would classify themselves as "Great Commission Christians." Therefore another perspective on the remaining task is necessary.

The "reached – unreached" graphic perspective (the individual metric)

Looking at the remaining task from the "reached – unreached" perspective sheds more light on the true spiritual condition at the individual level throughout the world. Uncannily, the word's population falls rather evenly into three distinct categories from this perspective. One-third are "reached," one-third "under-reached," and a final third "unreached." Notice the three divisions as follows:

World Population: 6.9 Billion

UNREACHED & UNSAVED No witnessing community within their people group or area 33% 2.3 billion	World "A" Very limited access to the gospel
UNDER-REACHED & UNSAVED Most have never had a clear presentation of the gospel, although it is nearby 33% 2.3 billion	World "B" Some access to the gospel
REACHED BUT NOT SAVED Some knowledge of the gospel, nominal acceptance 23% 1.6 billion - REACHED & SAVED – G.C. CHRISTIANS 11% 700 million	World "C" Access to the gospel[4]

When the task is looked at in this light, the reality can be rather disturbing. One of the metrics we noted for Great Commission progress was the "individual metric" (chapter 10). In accordance with Mark 16:15, if every human being is to have an opportunity to hear a clear presentation of the gospel, then close to two-thirds of the world's population are still awaiting that opportunity. Furthermore, the statistics placing the number of born-again believers in the world at 700 million, or 11% of the world's population could well be unrealistic (the World Evangelical Alliance puts the figure at around 420 million). Thankfully, this is up from a mere 3% in 1950. However, it also shows that the number who have yet to believe is 6.2 billion (89%) or 9 out of 10 people.

One of the best mission mottos that helps us understand the importance of reaching every individual is one popularized by the now disbanded AD2000 and Beyond Movement.[5] Their motto, "A Church for Every People, and the Gospel for Every Person," placed a well-founded focus on the importance of planting churches in every people group so that in turn every individual within that group would have opportunity to hear the gospel. This should continue to be our goal.

The geographic perspective (the geographical metric)

Of the three metrics given in the Great Commission, this one comes the closest to being realized. Truly, there is no country on earth where the church is not planted. According to the count of the United Nations, there are 236 geo-political "countries" in the world. Not one of them is without a church. In some, the church may be hidden or underground, but it is there. The gospel has reached the remotest "end of the earth" (Acts 1:8). The church is indeed global, and more solidly so than in anytime in history. The expansiveness of Christianity compared to other religions is evident.[6]

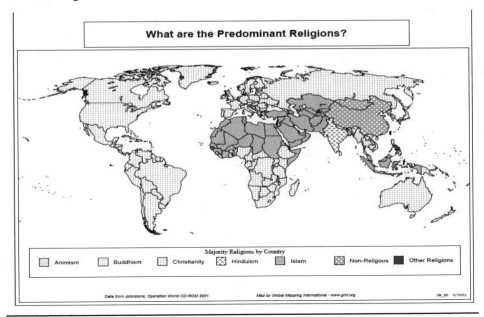

What are the Predominant Religions?

Majority Religions by Country

Animism   Buddhism   Christianity   Hinduism   Islam   Non-Religous   Other Religions

Data from Johnstone, Operation World CD-ROM 2001.   Map by Global Mapping International - www.gmi.org

Note that Asia is the only continent where Christianity is not the majority religion. However, Asia is our greatest challenge because of the preponderance of population that is there. If the world were drawn to population proportion, this is how it would look:[7]

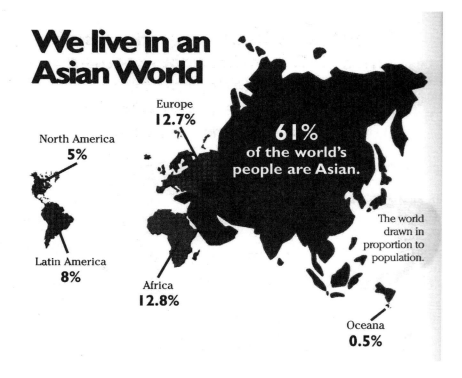

We live in an Asian World

Europe
12.7%

North America
5%

61%
of the world's
people are Asian.

The world
drawn in
proportion to
population.

Latin America
8%

Africa
12.8%

Oceana
0.5%

The people group perspective (the ethnical metric)

One last metric that comes from two Great Commission passages is the people group metric (Mt. 28:19, Lk. 24:47). As stated in chapter 4, the Lausanne Strategy Working Group in 1982 defined a people group to be:

> a significantly large grouping of individuals who perceive themselves to have a common affinity for one another because of their shared language, religion, ethnicity, residence, occupation, class or caste, situation, etc. or combinations of these...the largest group within which the Gospel can spread as a church planting movement without encountering barriers of understanding or acceptance.

Different terms have been used to define peoples who have yet to be fully evangelized. Some prefer the term "unreached," others "under-reached," and still others "least-reached." Although "unreached" has become the standard used in this discussion, "least reached" is rather popular and becoming more commonly used. One mission has defined "least reached" as, "people who do not have access to a church that preaches the gospel in their language and culture."[8]

The older definition of unreached peoples is very similar, but a little more exacting. In chapter 4, an unreached people group was identified as, "An ethno-linguistic people within which there is no viable indigenous church planting movement with sufficient strength, resources, and commitment to sustain and ensure the continuous multiplication of churches."[9] Or put another way, it is any group that does not contain a contextualized church demonstrably capable of completing the evangelization of that group.

The following are interesting facts about unreached people groups (UPGs) from a source that devotes itself fully to UPG research.[10]

- Of the 16,302 people groups by country, 6,649 are still considered least-reached / unreached.

- 9,653 people groups by country are NOT Least-Reached, totaling 3,920,483,000 individuals, or about 59% of the world's population.

- 1,444 of the Least-Reached groups are NOT in the 10/40 Window, totaling 350,929,000 individuals. These groups are relatively accessible to the Good News of the Gospel.

- Of the 6,649 Least-Reached people groups, about 3,460 (52%) are small groups under 10,000 in population (or population unknown) and all these groups total less than 8,000,000 individuals. Of the remaining 3,189 least-reached groups, about 1,302 are under 50,000 in population. That leaves 1,887 Least-Reached groups 50,000 and over in population. A vibrant church in a large group may take the gospel to a number of smaller satellite people groups that have ethnic similarities.

- Of the world's approximately 6,900 languages, 4,694 have at least one of the following: Bible portions, the Jesus Film, Christian radio, or gospel recordings. Total speakers of these languages is 6,200,000,000, or over 95% of the world's population.

- Of 236 total countries, 169 (72%) are Christian-majority countries. Total population for these countries is 2,517,000,000.

Almost every country of the world contains unreached people groups within it. The following shows the countries that have the greatest number of unreached/least-reached peoples:[11]

Country	Number of Peoples total	Number of Unreached Peoples
India	2501	2190
China	516	427
Pakistan	389	374
Bangladesh	400	353
Nepal	332	308

The importance of all three metrics

In his commission, Jesus gave a three-fold command relating to his mission's extension. Understanding the remaining task by way of these related metrics (individual, geographical, and ethnical) helps to bring a better understanding to not only what needs to be done but also where.

All three components need our simultaneous attention, and one should not be minimized in favor of another. The three are interrelated and are best thought of as relating to each other concentrically. As Christ's ambassadors move across

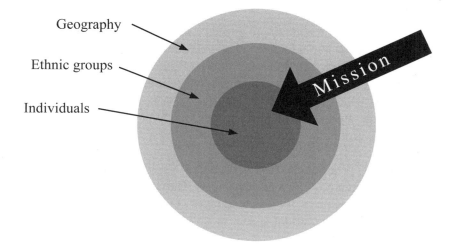

geographic boundaries, they enter ethnic groups and cultures, which in turn permit encounters with individuals within those groups so they might hear the message. This concentric concept is illustrated on the previous page.

What Jesus wants you to know as you go...

Through the centuries the Church, sending out hundreds of thousands of missionaries and expending billions upon billions of dollars, has engaged in the task of world evangelization. However, the task is still far from complete. When understood from the three metrics mentioned in the Great Commission, it becomes obvious that much remains undone.

Of the three metrics, the geographic metric is the one that is the closest to being achieved. However, that is only one of the three used to measure our progress. The ethnic metric shows that 40% of the world's people groups are still totally unreached and the individual metric indicates that 2.3 billion people have no witnessing community within their reach and are still awaiting a clear presentation of the gospel. One in four have never heard the gospel - not even once. It is easier to find a coke in the world than the gospel! There is still much to be done.

Chapter 12

The Great Commission and You

Have you stopped to consider what role God would have YOU play in accomplishing the Great Commission? Maybe that is why you read this book – because you are seeking to determine that for yourself. Possibly you have become so gripped with Jesus' command to "disciple the nations" that you are personally seeking how you might do that very thing.

Obedience to the teachings of Jesus is seldom easy. Obedience to his command to join in the work of his Great Commission can be even more difficult. To engage in it is not for the faint of heart or weak in spirit. On one level, it takes a combination of willingness, determination, faith and risk-taking for one to personally cross over into different cultures and possibly live on foreign soil to bring other peoples to the knowledge of Jesus Christ. On another level, it may simply mean helping those who commit to such a path, by rendering support services through the means of regular prayer, financial resources, material assistance, technical support, or moral encouragement. Being an obedient Great Commission Christian will take you down one of those two paths.

Whatever the path that is chosen, those who willingly engage find peace of heart and a settled mind in knowing they are doing what is dear to God. Can there be any more worthy cause than to engage in the mission of our Lord? Can there be any higher or nobler calling than to align one's will with his? Can there be a better spending of one's life, talents and resources other than in the service of the Great Commissioner?

Giving up one's small ambitions and selfish goals for eternal benefits should never be thought of as a waste. On the contrary, selfless sacrifice brings much eternal gain (Phil. 1:21). That is why Jim Elliot could confidently say, "He is no fool who gives what he cannot keep to gain what he cannot lose." There are no losers in the work of God, especially when bringing people to saving faith in Christ.

The responsibility of world evangelization was not lost on past generations. Samuel Mills, who was instrumental in propelling America into missions, at the famous "Haystack prayer meeting" in 1806, challenged a small band of fellow students with the now famous words, "We can do it, if we will." When you stop to think about it, that axiom can be taken two different ways: having the will to act, and deliberately taking action.

Today, the Church has all the resources at its disposal to finish the task. We have more and better educated people, more financial resources, more material resources, and more technological resources available to us than any previous generation. However, the one thing most lacking, the thing in which believers today seem most deficient, is *the will to act*. We cannot do it if we *will* not!

What others have said

If you feel hesitant to engage in some meaningful way in the Great Commission, then consider what others have said who have gone before us.[1]

God has called enough men and women to evangelize all the yet unreached tribes of the earth. Why do I believe that? Because everywhere I go, I constantly meet with men and women who say to me, "When I was young I wanted to be a missionary, but I got married instead," or, "My parents dissuaded me," or some such thing. No it is not God who does not call. It is man who will not respond.

– Isobel Kuhn

As long as I see anything to be done for God, life is worth living; but O how vain and unworthy it is to live any lower end!

– David Brainerd

It is conceivable that God might have ordained to preach the gospel directly to man through dreams, visions, and revelations. But as a matter of fact he has not done this, but rather has committed the preaching to man, telling them to go and disciple all nations. The responsibility lies squarely on our shoulders.

– J. Osward Sanders

How do Christians discharge this trust committed to them? They let three-fourths of the world sleep the sleep of death, ignorant of the simple truth that a Savior died for them. Content if they can be useful in the little circle of their acquaintances, they quietly sit and see whole nations perish for the lack of knowledge.

– Adoniram Judson

Let us remind ourselves that the Great Commission was never qualified by clauses calling for advance only if funds were plentiful and no hardship or self-denial involved. On the contrary, we are told to expect tribulation and even persecution, but with it victory in Christ...It is ours to show, in the salvation of our Lord Jesus Christ, and in personal communion with him, a joy unspeakable and full of glory that cannot be affected by outside circumstances.

– John Stam

The motto of every missionary, whether preacher, printer, or school master ought to be "devoted for life."

– Adoniram Judson

To know the will of God we need an open Bible and an open map.

– William Carey

...if God has called you to China or any other place and you are sure in your own heart, let nothing deter you...remember it is God who has called you and it is the same as when He called Moses or Samuel.

– Gladys Aylward

If Jesus Christ be God and died for me, then no sacrifice can be too great for me to make for Him.

– C.T. Studd

The Great Commission is not an option to be considered; it is a command to be obeyed.

– J. Hudson Taylor

One final question

There is only one question remaining when it comes to the Great Commission: what part are *you willing* to have? Are you willing to engage it with passion and intention? Are you willing to be devoted for life? If you cannot do so by going, can you commit to a supporting role? While it is true that God does not call all to go, he does call all to grow in a deeper understanding of his mission and then be a part of it in accordance to their capabilities. The support team is just as vital to The Cause as those who are serving on the front lines.

John Woodbridge asks, "What higher commission could a human being have than to be Christ's ambassador, His personal representative? Amazingly enough, that is the very mission to which each one of us as a Christian has been called: to be an ambassador for Christ. We are all on an awesome assignment in this life."[2]

> If missions languish, it is because the whole life of godliness is feeble. The command to go everywhere and preach to everybody is not obeyed until the will is lost by self-surrender in the will of God. Living, praying, giving and going will always be found together.
> - Arthur T. Pierson

Yes, to be an ambassador for Christ, to join his Cause by way of the Great Commission, is what he asks of each of us. No believer should ever feel that he or she is exempt. Jesus will not excuse those who refuse to play even a small part. A widow's mite is just as valuable as a missionary onsite.

A final thought from a noted mission historian brings this discussion and book to a close:

In seeking to fulfill Jesus' command, his disciples will not always succeed. They will not always be able to persuade others; their judgment will be faulty; they will not be fully free from the taint of sin; physical weakness will thwart them; what men call death will come, early or late, to cut off the act before its final accomplishment, so far beyond the compass of human years has it been planned. Yet it is through daring to live now in the new age and not resting content until all their fellow creatures share it that God brings in his Kingdom. He is not ashamed to be called their God. In the eternity beyond this present span, we must believe, they will not be disappointed for they have ventured out in faith in him who is 'able to do far more abundantly than all that we ask or think.'[3]

Indeed, over the past two millennia, myriads of Christ-followers have ventured out in faith, joining Christ in his redemptive mission to mankind. They exercised the boldness to do so based on a firm conviction that Jesus' commission was meant personally for them. And, like them, so can you! His instructions are clear and precise. There is little danger in misinterpreting the nature of the task. Everything you need to *know as you go* is found in the Great Commission commands of Christ. Place them at the center of your mission, vision and passion, and you will not go wrong as you go forth. So go! Go in the confidence that you are doing what he has intended to be done. You too have been commissioned.

> When all has been said that can be said on this issue, the greatest remaining mystery is not the character of God nor the destiny of lost people. The greatest mystery is why those who are charged with rescuing the lost have spent two thousand years doing other things, good things, perhaps, but have failed to send and be sent until all have heard the liberating word of life in Christ Jesus. The lost condition of human beings breaks the Father's heart. What does it do to ours?
>
> – Robertson McQuilkin

End Notes

Preface

[1] The origin of the term "Great Commission" is difficult to ascertain. According to missiologist David Hesselgrave, one of the first written occurrences of the term was by Pope Paul III in 1537. Following that, various other writers used the term down to the Moravians, where it entered Protestant circles. However, it was William Carey who popularized the term in Protestantism, making the argument in 1792 that the commission applied to all believers. (David Hesselgrave, "Great Commission," Evangelical Dictionary of World Missions, p. 413.) The term has become so common that it is now a subtitle located somewhere in Matthew 28 in most English versions of the Bible.

[2] Encarta® World English Dictionary© 1999 Microsoft Corporation. All rights reserved. Developed for Microsoft by Bloomsbury Publishing.

[3] Ibid.

[4] George Peters observes that the "Great Commission as recorded in the various gospels belongs to the living tradition of the church of the apostles." The very fact that all writers of the gospels cite it in one form or another is clear evidence that its existence and content were quite universally known. George Peters, A Biblical Theology of Missions, p. 132.

[5] J. Herbert Kane. Christian Missions in Biblical Perspective, pp. 43-44.

[6] John Stott, "The Great Commission," One Race, One Gospel, One Task. Vol.1, ed. C.F.H. Henry and W.S. Mooneyham, p.37.

[7] This is the opinion of Robert Hall Glover a missiologist who had a great influence on the Evangelical faith movement in the 1920s-40s. This quote is take from his book The Bible Basis of Missions, p. 25.

[8] A fresh articulation of appropriate mission activities coupled with their relation to Christ's authorization to our mission goals based on these statements is well overdue. Christopher Wright correctly observes: "I believe 21st century missiology will have to wrestle with the doctrine of Scripture that moves beyond the way Evangelical scholarship has tended to defend the inspiration and authority of the Bible with the concepts and methods of modernity itself, towards a more dynamic understanding of the authority and role of the Bible in a post-modern world. And I think this will be one the biggest challenges for Christian theology in the 21st century, since there is no mission without the authority of Christ himself, and our access to that authority depends upon the Scriptures. So a major missiological task for Evangelical theology will be a fresh articulation of the authority of the Bible and its relation to Christ's authorization of our mission." Chris Wright. *Global Missiology For The 21st Century*. William D. Taylor, editor, p.76.

[9] This is in reference to the "Nazareth Manifesto" of Luke 4 that is gaining in popularity, which will be discussed in chapter 8.

Chapter 1

[1] George Peters in *A Biblical Theology of Missions,* seems to prefer this term, p. 212, because it gives the charter to the church's responsibility in her outward relationship.

[2] The timing of Luke's commission is the most difficult to ascertain. However, most commentators would agree that there is a division of time between Luke 24:43 and what follows starting with verse 44. A reading of the text would suggest that verses 44-49 would have taken place back in Jerusalem after the disciples had met with Jesus in Galilee. Alexander Bruce in *The Expositor's Greek Testament*, commenting on this section from Luke states, "It is at this point, if anywhere, that room must be made for an extended period of occasional intercourse between Jesus and His disciples. It is conceivable that what follows refers to another occasion" (page 650). Henry Alford agrees, with the added emphasis that these words "cannot have been said on this evening; for after the command in verse 49, the disciples would not have gone away into Galilee, (page 673).

Chapter 2

[1] A related phrase, "The Living God is a Missionary God", comes from John Stott, the title of his article in *Perspectives On the World Christian Movement*, pp. 3-9.

[2] See *Transforming Mission*, p.1-2, where David Bosch makes the argument that these four components are logically necessary part of any sending, and that the traditional concept of mission is under attack today, not only from without but also from within the church.

[3] For a fuller discussion on the Old Testament concept of centripetal focus and the New Testament concept of the opposite centrifugal focus, see George Peters, *A Biblical Theology of Missions*, pp. 21-22.

[4] The tense of the first "sent" *apostello* is aorist, showing an action once taken and not to be repeated. Jesus was sent only once into the world to provide salvation for mankind. The second "send" *pempo* is present tense, something that keeps going on, intended to show a sending that keeps going until the job is completed.

[5] One of the best books on leadership practices is by Kouzes and Posner, *The Leadership Challenge*. Modeling the way is the first of five basic leadership practices of a good leader.

[6] This is what is asserted by James Engel and William Dyrness when they mistakenly chose to ignore the Great Commission passages and land on Luke 4:18-19 as the defining passage for mission both in Jesus'

ministry and for all missionaries today. Their error of ignoring the obvious, clear Great Commission mission passages and elevating the obscure is a classical hermeneutical mistake that finds little justification.

[7] Andreas J Kostenberger and Peter T. O'Brien, *Salvation to the Ends of the Earth.* p.169 ff.

[8] Christopher Little, "What Makes Mission Christian?" in *International Journal of Frontier Missiology.* April-June 2008:65-73.

[9] In Hebrews 3:1 Jesus is called "the apostle." An apostle is one who is sent on an official mission. He is in our terms, a missionary – the Latin equivalent and translation of the word *apostle.* Therefore, Jesus is himself called a missionary in the New Testament.

[10] This was the position of noted British theologian John Stott, who influenced many to take this position. Stott changed his mind from an earlier position he held, namely that the commissions contained the priority of evangelistic responsibility over social responsibility. Following the 1974 Lausanne Conference on World Evangelization (LCWE), Stott went so far as to quickly publish a short book entitled *Christian Mission in the Modern World,* In it he states, "I now see more clearly that not only the consequences of the commission but the actual commission itself must be understood to include social as well as evangelistic responsibility, unless we are to be guilty of distorting the words of Jesus," p.23. In Stott's view, the "as the Father sent me, so send I you" indicates a strong parallel between Jesus' mission and ours by the model of Jesus.

Others, like Engel and Dyrness, in *Changing The Mind of Missions,* chose to ignore all five of the Great Commission passages altogether, finding them inadequate to justify their bias for social concern as a part of mission. Instead, they put forward Luke 4:18-19 (what has since been called the "Nazareth Manifesto") as the commission we are to follow as our model in mission. This position will be discussed further in chapter 8.

Chapter 3

[1] Henry Alford in his commentary, *The Greek Testament,* states this about the word "creature." "Not to men only, all creation is redeemed by Christ (Col. 1:15,23) "creature" never appears in the NT to be used of mankind alone. By these words the missionary office is bound upon the church through all ages, till every part of the earth shall have been evangelized," p.437.

[2] For a fuller discussion of how both Catholic and Protestant missions are "greening," see Allan Effa's article "The Greening of Mission" in *International Bulletin of Missionary Research*, Vol. 32, No.4, October 2008. The accompanying article "Missiology in Environmental Context: Tasks for an Ecology of Mission," by Willis Jenkins is also helpful in seeing the current popular trend of linking eco-mission into the Church's mission. Disappointingly, both articles are examples of how the Great Commission passages are ignored in this discussion.

[3] Patrick Johnstone in *The Church is Bigger Than You Think*, argues that this passage as well as others would be better translated "evangelize." He bemoans the fact that the common Greek form is too often translated, "preach the gospel" or "tell the good news," distorting the real force that texts like Mark 16:15 show that the church's real task is to evangelize (p.47-48).

[4] www.lausanne.org/lausanne-1974/lausanne-covenant.html.

[5] www.preachhim.org/poempage.htm.

[6] Corrie, John. Faith to Faith Forum: "Is Evangelism a Sin?" www.globalconnections.co/uk/ftof

[7] Ibid.

Chapter 4

[1] Patrick Johnstone, *The Church is Bigger Than You Think.* pp 53-54.

[2] J. Herbert Kane, *Christian Missions in Biblical Perspective.* p. 149.

[3] Terry, Smith, Anderson, *Missiology.* pp. 71-72.

[4] Adopted and modified from Craig Blomberg, *A Survey of the Life of Christ.* p. 357.

[5] Robert E. Coleman, *The Master Plan of Evangelism.* p.173.

[6] George Barna, *Growing True Disciples.* Colorado Springs: Waterbook Press, 2001.

[7] George Peters, *A Biblical Theology of Missions.* p. 189.

[8] Terry, Smith, Anderson, ibid. p. 72.

[9] Craig Blomberg, ibid. p.356.

[10] Terry, Smith, Anderson, p. 73.

[11] Senior and Stuhlmueller observe that, "Missionary proclamation includes the formation of a community, or 'church.' This is the implication of Matthew's use of the baptismal formula in 28:19. Such ecclesiastical interest harmonizes with the whole tone of Matthew's gospel. The ekklesia (or "church") that gathers in Jesus' name (c.f.16:18, 18:17,20) is the place where the values of the kingdom are to be manifested: mercy, compassion, reconciliation." p. 252.

[12] John Piper, *Let the Nations Be Glad!* p. 171.

[13] www.joshuaproject.net/great-commission-statistics.php.

[14] Patrick Johnstone, ibid. p. 104.

[15] "*The Breast-plate of St. Patrick,*" http://www.theseason.org/breast.htm.

[16] Charles Spurgeon, *The Gospel of Matthew.* p. 416.

Chapter 5

[1] Eugene Nida in *Meaning Across Culture* deals extensively with this topic. Although an older anthropological work, Nida's observations about meaning in culture still hold true today.

[2] Animists are those who believe that the world around them is pulsating with unseen menacing spirits. These spirits need to be appeased if they are not to cause harm, injury or even death. Although tribal peoples are most steeped in these beliefs, elements of animism are found in all of the major world religions to one degree or another. New Age channelers and Spiritists hold to the identical basic beliefs.

[3] Winfried Corduan, *Neighboring Faiths*. pp. 45-46.

[4] Harold Dollar, "Resurrection of Christ" in *Evangelical Dictionary of World Missions*. p. 827.

[5] Bill Thrasher, "Repentance" in *Evangelical Dictionary of World Missions*. p. 824.

[6] W.E. Vine, *An Expository Dictionary of New Testament Words*. pp. 122-123.

[7] The unpublished SEND "Salvation of the Unevangelized" statement, on the lost, states this as clearly as any statement: "The clear statements of Scripture teach that all men are sinners by nature, choice and practice (Rom. 3:9-19;5:12). All people are under God's wrath and judgment because their sin is an affront to God's perfect holiness (Rom. 1:18; 2:5-6; 1 Pet. 1:16). All people deserve the judgment of God because of their inherited and willful sin (Rom. 6:23)." (IC '96/SEND International).

Chapter 6

[1] Robert Hall Glover, *The Bible Basis of Missions*. p.70.

[2] Engle and Dyrness in *Changing The Mind of Missions*, p.69. In this regard Engel and Dyrness say "...it quickly can lead to the seductive temptation to reduce world missions to a manageable enterprise – with a large hierarchical structure to carry it out. Samuel Escabar has coined the phrase 'managerial missiology' to refer to an unduly pragmatic endeavor to reduce reality to an understandable picture, and then to project missionary action as a response to a problem that has been described in quantitative form."

[3] John Stott, *Christian Mission in the Modern World*, p. 125.

[4] Ibid.

[5] John Stott, *The Message of Acts*, p.33. Stott is of the opinion that the title "Acts of the Holy Spirit" over-emphasizes the divine and overlooks the apostles as the chief characters through whom the Spirit worked. His suggestion of a better title would be "The Continuing Words and Deeds of Jesus by his Spirit through the Apostles."

[6] George Peters. *A Biblical Theology of Missions*. p. 214. Peters also added this important note, (p. 213-214), "Since the Christian life is charged with supernatural ideals and demands, it can only believe in absolute reliance on the Holy Spirit. Unless the lessons are learned early, the Christian life becomes beset with frustrations and numbness; apathy sets in, or people become conditioned to an abnormal or subnormal Christian life. This is the tragedy of countless believers who do not even expect to live up to the biblical ideals."

[7] Lamin Sanneh, *Disciples of All Nations: Pillars of World Christianity*. p.13-14. Sanneh adds, "As the ancient scribe foresaw, in the age of true religion God's name would no longer be confined to one place but would be known and honored everywhere among the Gentiles. The witness of believers that God was their only dwelling place has been validated."

[8] As the events in the book of Acts unfolded, Luke informs us of the springing up of regional centers of Christianity. Although Jerusalem held the distinction as the sole center of the church for 20 years, by the middle of the book, Antioch is mentioned as a strong center (by the AD 50's). Towards the end of the book, Ephesus is a growing center of influence (AD 60's), with the hint of Rome emerging on the scene as an upcoming center.

[9] Ralph D. Winter and Steven C. Hawthorne, editors, *Perspectives on the World Christian Movement, A Reader*. pp. 339-353.

[10] Ibid., p.345. For a fuller discussion by Dr. Ralph Winter on the implications of the three kinds of evangelism, read his entire address in *Perspectives*. Winter brings up the issue of "people blindness" that relates directly to the unfinished task.

[11] Carey wrote these words in his 87-page pamphlet *An Enquiry into the Obligation of Christians to Use Means for the Conversion of the Heathens* in 1792. His arguments were convincing enough that the Particular Baptist agreed to set up a sending agency, Baptist Missionary Society (first of its kind in the English-speaking world), and send him and his wife Dorothy as their first missionaries to India the following year.

[12] J. Herbert Kane, *Christian Missions in Biblical Perspective*. p. 54.

[13] Definition of David Barrett, cited by Karen White in "Overcoming Resistance through Martyrdom," J. Dudley Woodbury, editor. *Reaching the Resistant*. Evangelical Missiological Society Series, No. 6. Pasadena: William Carey Library, 1998.

Chapter 7

[1] This definition takes several important aspects of sending into account. One would be that the origin of the sending, although from God, is affirmed by believers of the church. Another is that those truly of missionary status are those who go cross-culturally, beyond the borders of their own culture. A third aspect is that they go where the gospel is either unknown, or not believed if it is already known.

[2] George Peters sees the authorization as being so important that he places the word right in his definition: "A messenger with a message from God, sent forth by divine authority for the definite purpose of evangelism, church–founding and church edification" (*A Biblical Theology of Missions*, p. 248).

[3] www.desiringgod.org/ResourceLibrary/Articles/ByDate/2006/1442.

[4] Christian A. Schwarz, *The 3 Colors of Ministry*. pp 10-14.

[5] Huntington, *Clash of civilizations*. The Clash of Civilizations is a theory, proposed by political scientist Samuel P. Huntington, that people's cultural and religious identities will be the primary source of conflict in the post-Cold War world. The theory was originally formulated in a 1992 lecture at the American Enterprise Institute, which was then developed in a 1993 Foreign Affairs article titled "The Clash of Civilizations?" in response to Francis Fukuyama's 1992 book, *The End of History and the Last Man*. Huntington later expanded his thesis in a 1996 book *The Clash of Civilizations and the Remaking of World Order*. (http://en.wikipedia.org/wiki/Clash_of_Civilizations).

[6] In his book *Through God's Eyes* (pp. 51-53), Patrick Cate suggests this exercise as a way of helping believers understand the essence of the gospel, using 25 words or less.

[7] Some of these summaries are taken from Theology of Missions class notes presented by Dr. John Orme at Moody Graduate School.

[8] This axiom has been attributed to Anglican bishop Lesslie Newbigin.

[9] J.D. Payne says it well: "Biblical church planting follows the way modeled by Jesus and imitated by the Apostolic Church for global disciple-making. It is a methodology and a strategy for bringing in the harvest, raising up leaders from the harvest, and sending leaders to work in the harvest fields. It is evangelism resulting in congregationalizing. Under the leadership and work of the Holy Spirit, biblical church planting seeks to trans-

late the gospel and the irreducible ecclesiological minimum into any given social context, with the expectation that new communities of believers in turn will continue the process in their contexts and throughout the world." (In Thom S. Rainer and Chuck Lawless, *The Challenge of the Great Commission* (n.p. Pinnacle Publishing), pp. 107-108).

[10] Lesslie Newbigin, *The Household of God.* (SCM, 1953), p. 25.

[11] "William Whiting Borden," http://en.wikipedia.org/wiki/William_Whiting_Borden.

[12] Dr. and Mrs. Howard Taylor, *By Faith*: Henry W. Frost and the China Inland Mission, p. 299.

Chapter 8

[1] Steven Neill, *Creative Tension.* p. 81.

[2] Herbert Kane, *The Christian World Mission: Today and Tomorrow.* pp.153-54. Also, noted missiologist, David Hesselgrave, suggests that holism is already included in Matthew 28:16-20. "That passage clearly presents the very 'holism' or universals intrinsic to biblical mission: 'all authority,' 'all nations or peoples,' 'all things whatsoever I have commanded,' and 'I am with you always.' If we want to preserve the term 'holistic mission,' we can do no better than return to the priority and meaning that our Lord himself ascribes to it." "Redefining Holism," in *Evangelical Missions Quarterly* July 1999, Vol. 35, No. 3 p. 282.

[3] George Peters, *A Biblical Theology of Missions.* p. 168.

[4] Gordon Olson, *Beyond Calvinism and Arminianism*, page 281. Olson quotes Thomas Helwys of the Particular Baptists who in 1611 wrote that this position, "...makes some despair utterly as thinking there is not grace for them and that God hath decreed their destruction. And it makes other desperately careless, holding that if God have decreed they shall be saved then they shall be saved, and if God have decreed they shall be damned, they shall be damned."

[5] Ibid. p.383.

[6] Richard Fletcher, *Barbarian Conversion: from Paganism to Christianity.* p 1.

[7] An advocate of this view was from Lutheran theologian Johann Ursinius. He not only cited this as a reason not to engage in the Great Commission, but also the difficulty of recruiting missionaries and the deep depravity of the heathen making them next to impossible to convert.

[8] Engel and Dyrness, *Changing the Mind of Missions.* pp. 21-25.

[9] *Encarta® World English Dictionary©* 1999 Microsoft Corporation. All rights reserved. Developed for Microsoft by Bloomsbury Publishing.

[10] Engel and Dyrness, ibid. p.27. This is what Engel & Dyrness suggest they are doing, and in actuality is the thesis of their book.

Chapter 9

[1] This is literally true. When visiting in northern Cameroon with a group of graduate students, we were invited into the palace of "the Fonz", king of Okuland. He was a Christian king, and a former pastor. There on the center of the wall behind his throne in bold letters was John 3:16 fully written out.

[2] University of Florida quarterback Tim Tebow, a missionary kid, devout believer, and arguably the best college quarterback ever in the history of the game, etched "John" under one eye and "3:16" under the other in the 2008 FedEx BCS National Championship bowl. It was not hard for television cameras to pick it up, and believers around the country were thrilled to see this bold testimony.

[3] Timothy George. "Big-Picture Faith" in *Christianity Today*. October 23, 2000.

[4] This can be said categorically because of the theology contained therein. Of the nine divisions of systematic theology, five are mentioned: 1) Theology proper, "God" as the source of salvation; 2) Anthropology, "world" (since man is the apex of the created order) the object of salvation; 3) Christology, "his Son" the means of salvation, 4) Soteriology, "whoever believes" the appropriation of salvation; and 5) eschatology, "not perish but have eternal life," the benefit of salvation.

[5] Erich Saurer, *The Dawn of World Redemption*, translated by G.H. Lang (1951), p.85.

[6] LaTonya Taylor, "The Church of O," *Christianity Today*. April 1, 2002.

[7] John Piper, *Let the Nations Be Glad!* Grand Rapids: Baker Academic, 2003, p. 141.

[8] John Stott in his honesty struggled with this concept. "Emotionally, I find the concept (of eternal conscious punishment) intolerable and do not understand how people can live with it without either cauterizing their feelings or cracking under the strain. David Edwards, *Evangelical Essentials*, with a Response from John Stott. Downers Grove: InterVarsity Press, 1988, pp.314-320.

[9] This is the view of Clark Pinnock in "Fire, Then Nothing." *Christianity Today*, 44, no. 10 (20 March 1987):49.

[10] This summary is taken from *Through No Fault of Their Own?: The Fate of Those Who Have Never Heard* by William V. Crockett and James G. Sigountos, 1991 pp.23-24.

[11] www.wow4u.com/mousetrap

[12] Ron Blue in *Evangelism and Missions*, pp. 81-82, notes that denial of this truth threatens every area of theology:
1. The character of God (theology proper) is questioned: "Is God just?"
2. The sufficiency of Christ (Christology) is questioned: "Is Christ the only way?"
3. The necessity of the cross (soteriology) is questioned: "Did Christ have to die?"
4. The depravity of man (anthropology) is questioned: "Is man inherently sinful?"
5. The judgment of sin (hamartiology) is questioned: "Is not evil relative?"
6. The role of the church (ecclesiology) is questioned: "Does it need to witness?"
7. The finale of history (eschatology) is questioned: "Is there a future reckoning?"
To these I would add two more to round out the classical nine:
8. The work of the Holy Spirit (pneumatology) is questioned: "Does he need to convict the world of sin, righteousness and judgment?

9. The authority of Scripture (bibliology) is questioned: "Can the Bible be believed in regard to the matter of man's predicament and God's solution?

Chapter 10

[1] David Bosch, *Transforming Mission*. p.1.

[2] Bill Schuit, "The Relay" in *Currents*. Published by Leibenzell USA, Sept/Oct 2008.

[3] Frances Hesselbein, *Hesselbein on Leadership*. pp. 41-42.

[4] Camille F. Bishop, *We're in This Boat Together*. p. 161.

[5] The sources consulted for these histories are: H.S. Vigeveno *Thirteen Men Who Changed the World*. Glendale, CA: Regal Books, 1969, and www.ccel.org/bible/phillips/CN500APOSTLES%FATE.htm.

Chapter 11

[1] These statistics are based on tables supplied by David Barrett, Todd Johnson, and Peter Crossing in the article, "Christian World Communions: Five Overviews of Global Christianity, AD 1800-2025" in the mission journal *International Bulletin of Missionary Research*, Vol.33, No 1. 2009, p. 32.

[2] Adapted from Thomas Schirrmacher. *International Journal for Religious Freedom*. Vol.1, Issue 1, 2008. pp.16-18.

[3] I am indebted to Patrick Johnstone for giving these in broad categories in his book *The Church is Bigger Than You Think*.

[4] David Barrett defines these categories as follows: World C – all persons who individually are Christians anywhere in the world. This is Christianity in its broadest expression and includes Roman Catholic, Orthodox. Protestant, Anglican, Evangelical and all derived or deviant forms of Christianity; World B – all non-Christians who have heard the gospel, or who live within societies and areas where they were or are likely to hear it during their lifetime; these are evangelized non-Christians; World A – all non-Christians who are unevangelized and likely to remain so without a new effort by Christians to take the gospel to them. Quoted by Patrick Johnstone, pp.67-68.

[5] Quoting from the now static AD2000 and Beyond website: "A Church for Every People and the Gospel for Every Person." The Great Commission is a two-fold command. In Matthew 28:19,20 Jesus commands us to "Go and make disciples of all nations (peoples)". The focus is to establish disciples in mature fellowships among every people group. In Mark 16:15 Jesus gave the task of preaching the gospel to every person. The focus here is to present the Gospel to every individual. The watchword of "a church for every people and the Gospel for every person" sums up this two-fold command. www.ad2000.org/status.htm.

[6] Jason Mandryk, "State of the Gospel", 2006 from a slide presentation based on research for *Operation World*.

[7] Patrick O. Cate, *Through God's Eyes*. p.62.

[8] This definition comes from the mission Christar, which focuses on reaching the least reached peoples of the earth.

[9] Patrick Johnstone, *The Church is Bigger Than You Think*. p. 104.

[10] Taken from Joshua Project: www.joshuaproject.net/great-commission-statistics.php.

[11] Ibid.

Chapter 12

[1] Many of these quotes are taken from *Through God's Eyes*, by Patrick O. Cate.

[2] John D. Woodbridge, *Ambassadors for Christ*. pp.10-11.

[3] Kenneth Scott Latourette, *These Sought a Country.* p.147.

Bibliography

Alford, Henry. *The Greek Testament*. Chicago: Moody Press, 1958.

Arias, Mortimer. *The Great Commission: Biblical Models for Evangelism*. Nashville: Abington Press, 1992.

Banks, William. *In Search of the Great Commission*. Chicago: Moody Press, 1991.

Barna, George. *Growing True Disciples*. Colorado Springs: Waterbook Press, 2001.

Barrett, David, Todd Johnson, and Peter Crossing. *Christian World Communions: Five Overviews of Global Christianity, AD 1800-2025*. International Bulletin of Missionary Research, Vol.33, No 1, 2009.

Bridges, Jerry and Bob Bevington. *The Bookends of the Christian Life*. Wheaton: Crossway Books, 2009.

Bishop, Camille F. *We're in This Boat Together*. Colorado Springs: Authentic, 2008.

Blomberg, Craig L. *Jesus and the Gospels*. Nashville: Broadman & Holman Publishers, 1997.

Blue, Ron. *Evangelism and Missions*. Nashville: Word Publishing, 2001.

Bosch, David J. *Transforming Mission*. New York: Orbis Books, 1993.

Bruce, Alexander Balmain. *The Expositor's Greek Testament*. Grand Rapids: Wm. B. Eerdmans Publishing Company, 1974.

Cate, Patrick O. *Through God's Eyes*. Pasadena: William Carey Library, 2004.

Coleman, Robert E. *The Master Plan of Evangelism*, 30th anniversary edition. Grand Rapids: Fleming H. Revell, 1993.

Corduan, Winfried. *Neighboring Faiths*. Downers Grove: InterVarsity Press, 1998.

Corrie, John. Faith to Faith Forum: "Is Evangelism Ever a Sin." www.globalconnections.co.uk/ftof

Crockett, William V. and James G. Sigountos, eds. *Through No Fault of Their Own? The Fate of Those Who Have Never Heard*. Grand Rapids: Baker, 1991.

Dowsett, Rose. *The Great Commission*. Grand Rapids: Monarch Books, 2001.

Edwards, David. *Evangelical Essentials, with a Response from John Stott*. Downers Grove: InterVarsity Press, 1988.

Effa, Allen. T*he Greening of Mission. International Bulletin of Missionary Research*, Vol. 32, No.4, October 2008.

Encarta® World English Dictionary © 1999 Microsoft Corporation. All rights reserved. Developed for Microsoft by Bloomsbury Publishing.

Engel, James F. & William A. Dyrness. *Changing The Mind of Missions*. Downers Grove: InterVarsity Press, 2000.

Fletcher, Richard. *Barbarian Conversion: from Paganism to Christianity*. New York: Henry Holt, 1997.

Gallagher, Robert L. and Paul Hertig, editors. *Mission in Acts: Ancient Narratives in Contemporary Context*. New York: Orbis Books, 2004.

Gentry, Kenneth L. Jr. *The Greatness of the Great Commission*. Tyler, TX.: Institute For Christian Economics, 1990.

George, Timothy. "Big-Picture Faith" in *Christianity Today*. October 23, 2000.

Glover, Robert Hall. *The Bible Basis of Missions*. Los Angeles: Bible House of Los Angeles, 1946.

Harris, John. *The Great Commission or The Christian Church Constituted and Charged to Convey the Gospel to the World*. Boston: Gould, 1848.

Hesselbein, Frances. *Hesselbein on Leadership*. San Francisco: Jossey-Bass, 2002.

Hesselgrave, David. "Redefining Holism," *Evangelical Missions Quarterly*. July 1999, Vol. 35, No. 3. pp.278-284.

Howard, David M. *The Great Commission for Today*. Downers Grove: InterVarsity Press, 1976.

Johnstone, Patrick. *The Church is Bigger Than You Think*. Great Britain: Christian Focus Publications, 1998.

Kane, J. Herbert. *Christian Missions in Biblical Perspective*. Grand Rapids: Baker Book House, 1976.

The Christian World Mission: Today and Tomorrow. Grand Rapids: Baker Book House, 1981.

Klauber, Martin I. and Scott M. Maetsch. *The Great Commission: Evangelicals and the History of World Missions*. Nashville: B&H Academic, 2008.

Kostemberger, Andreas J. and Peter T. O'Brien. *Salvation to the Ends of the Earth*. Downers Grove: InterVarsity Press, 2001.

Kouzes, James M. and Barry Z. Posner. *Leadership Challenge*, Third edition. San Francisco: Jossey-Bass, 2002.

Latourette, Kenneth Scott. *These Sought a Country*. New York: Harper and Brothers, 1950.

Little, Christopher. "What Makes Mission Christian." *International Journal of Frontier Missiology*. April-June, 2008.

Mandryk, Jason. "State of the Gospel." Slide presentation, 2006.

Moreau, A. Scott, editor. *Evangelical Dictionary of World Missions*. Grand Rapids: Baker Books, 2000.

Newbigin, Lesslie. *The Household of God.* (SCM, 1953).

Neill, Stephen. *Creative Tension*. London: Edinburgh Press, 1959, p.81.

Nicoll, W. Robertson, editor. Alexander Balman Bruce. *The Expositor's Greek Testament*. Grand Rapids: Wm. B. Eerdmans Publishing Company, 1974.

Nida, Eugene A., William D. Reyburn. *Meaning Across Culture*. Maryknoll, NY.: Orbis, 1981.

Olson, Gordon. *Beyond Calvinism and Arminianism*. Cedar Knolls, NJ: Global Gospel Publishers, 2002.

Pentecost, J. Dwight. *The Words and Works of Jesus Christ*. Grand Rapids: Zondervan Publishing House, 1981.

Peters, George. *A Biblical Theology of Missions*. Chicago: Moody Press, 1972.

Pinnock, Clark. "Fire, Then Nothing". *Christianity Today*, 44 no. 10, March 20, 1987.

Piper, John. *Let the Nations be Glad!* Grand Rapids: Baker Academic, 2003.

Rainer, Thom S. and Chuck Lawless, *The Challenge of the Great Commission* (n.p. Pinnacle Publishing) 107-108.

Sanneh, Lamin. *Disciples of All Nations: Pillars of World Christianity*. New York: Oxford University Press, 2008.

Saurer, Erich. *The Dawn of World Redemption*, translated by G.H. Lang, London: Paternoster, 1951.

Schirrmacher. Thomas. *International Journal for Religious Freedom*. Vol.1, Issue 1, 2008.

Schuit, Bill. "The Relay" in *Currents*. Newsletter by Leibenzell.USA, Sept/Oct 2008.

Senior, Donald and Carroll Stuhlmueller. *The Biblical Foundations for Mission*. Maryknoll: Orbis Books, 1989.

Spurgeon, Charles Haddon. *The Gospel of Matthew*. Grand Rapids: Fleming H. Revell, 1987.

Stam, Cornelius. *Our Great Commission – What is it?* Stevens Point, WI.: Worzella Publishing Company, 1974.

Stott, John R.W. *Christian Mission in the Modern World*. Downers Grove: InterVarsity Press, 1975.

"The Great Commission," *One Race, One Gospel, One Task*. Vol.1, ed. C.F.H. Henry and W.S. Mooneyham. Minneapolis: World Wide Publications, 1967.

The Message of Acts. Downers Grove: Inter-Varsity Press, 1990.

Taylor, Dr. and Mrs. Howard. *By Faith: Henry W. Frost and the China Inland Mission*, Singapore: OMF books, 1988.

Taylor, LaTonya. "The Church of O." *Christianity Today*, April 1, 2002.

Taylor, William D., ed. *Global Missiology for the 21st Century*. Grand Rapids: Baker Academic, 2000.

Terry, John Mark, Ebbie Smith, and Justice Anderson. *Missiology*. Nashville: Broadman, & Holman Publishers, 1998.

Van Rheenen, Gailyn. *Missions: Biblical Foundations & Contemporary Strategies*, Grand Rapids: Zondervan Publishing House, 1996.

Vigeveno, H.S. *Thirteen Men Who Changed the World*. Glendale, CA: Regal Books, 1969.

Vine, W.E. *An Expository Dictionary of New Testament Words*. Westwood, N.J.: Fleming H. Revell Company, 1966.

Walls, Andrew and Cathy Ross, editors. *Mission in the 21st Century*. London: Darton, Longman and Todd, 2008.

White, Karen. "Overcoming Resistance through Martyrdom", J. Dudley Woodbury, editor. *Reaching the Resistant*. Evangelical Missiological Society Series, Number 6. Pasadena: William Carey Library, 1998.

Winter, Ralph D. and Steven C. Hawthorne, editors. *Perspectives on the World Christian Movement, A Reader,* Third Edition. Pasadena: William Carey Library, 1999.

Wright, Christopher J. H. *The Mission of God*. Downers Grove: IVP Academic, 2006.

Internet Resources consulted:

www.ad2000.org/status.htm.

www.ccel.org/bible/phillips/CN500APOSTLES%FATE.htm.

www.desiringgod.org/ResourceLibrary/Articles/ByDate/2006/1442.

www.lausanne.org/lausanne-1974/lausanne-covenant.html.

www.joshuaproject.net/great-commission-statistics.php.

www.prayerguide.org.uk/stfrancis.htm.

www.preachhim.org/poempage.htm.

www.theseason.org/breast.htm.

www.wow4u.com/mousetrap/index.html.

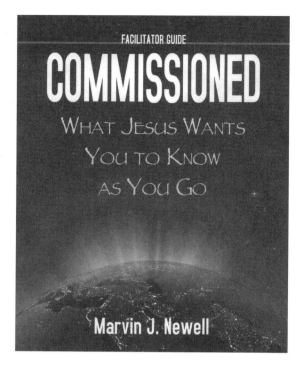

Now you can teach *Commissioned*!

Excellent for engaging small groups, adult Bible fellowships, Sunday School classes, mission committees and even Bible School classrooms.

The facilitator's guide includes:
- Lesson plans for either seven or twelve 50-minute sessions
- Facilitator's notes with filled-in answers for each session
- CD that includes:
  - ➤ Powerpoint to augment each session presentation
  - ➤ Participant Guide that can be duplicated for each participant
  - ➤ Colorful maps and charts

You need not be an expert on the Great Commission to teach *Commissioned*! Lesson plans are self-explanatory and easy to use.